The Random House Series in Money and Banking
Editor: Harlan M. Smith
University of Minnesota

THE ESSENTIALS OF MONEY AND BANKING
by Harlan M. Smith
University of Minnesota
A Core Volume (Clothbound)

INTERNATIONAL MONETARY RELATIONS
by Delbert Snider
Miami University, Oxford, Ohio
(paperback)

FINANCIAL INSTITUTIONS
by Raymond W. Goldsmith
Yale University
(paperback)

ELEMENTS OF MONETARY POLICY
by Thomas Mayer
University of California at Davis
(paperback)

ELEMENTARY MONETARY THEORY
by Harlan M. Smith
University of Minnesota
(paperback)

COMMERCIAL BANKING IN THE ECONOMY
by Paul Nadler
New York University
(paperback)

ELEMENTS OF
MONETARY POLICY

Elements
of
Monetary Policy

THOMAS MAYER

University of California at Davis

 RANDOM HOUSE *New York*

To Dorothy

Preface to the Series
by HARLAN M. SMITH

This series of books in money and banking has two primary purposes. First, it provides users of existing textbooks in the field with appropriate supplementary material in areas to which they may wish to devote additional attention. Second, in conjunction with the "core" volume (*The Essentials of Money and Banking* by Harlan M. Smith), this series makes it possible for each instructor and student in the field to put together a collection of books that will best suit his needs in terms of the amount of reading involved and the proportion of the course to be devoted to the different segments of the field. The core volume makes it possible to ensure that a basic minimum is covered in each of the areas traditionally included in money and banking courses. The "satellite" books may then be used to supplement the basic text in desired areas. The series thus provides a maximum degree of flexibility in selecting textbook materials for money and banking courses.

These books can serve other purposes as well, for each one is written in such a manner that it can be used independently, or in any desired combination, by anyone possessing an interest in its subject. The books provide, in every case, systematic expositions of their subjects, yet each is short enough to serve as supplementary text material in various courses as well as in the standard money and banking courses.

Preface

This book is a shorter version of my *Monetary Policy in the United States*. In writing it I had to choose among several ways to approach monetary policy. One is to emphasize history by discussing the origin and evolution of our present central bank and the actions it has taken in various years. The other is to focus on an evaluation of monetary policy by discussing the advantages and disadvantages of monetary policy as a stabilization tool. Within a short book one cannot use both approaches adequately, and I have chosen the latter. This one has the advantage of dealing with currently relevant issues rather than with the issues of the past. It does, however, have one disadvantage—the problems discussed in this book are still unsettled. I have tried to present both sides of the numerous debates, with the result that the reader may find himself in the position of the businessman who wanted to hire a one-armed economist since he was tired of hearing the man's predecessor say, "on the one hand . . . but on the other hand." However, these qualifications cannot be helped. Monetary policy is a field in which economists have achieved very considerable insight but little agreement. To pretend that there is agreement by presenting primarily one point of view would be less than candid. Similarly, to avoid controversial problems by ignoring them and discussing instead such "factual" material as changes in the Federal Reserve Act would give the reader little perspective on current problems. Having to choose among the three risks of being bewildering, less than candid, or irrelevant, I chose the first of these risks. I am dealing with unsettled issues because the unsettled issues are, unfortunately, the significant ones.

As far as background is concerned, I am assuming that the reader has some familiarity with monetary institutions —for example, that he knows something about the structure of the Federal Reserve System and the factors that increase or decrease bank reserves—and that he has had a limited exposure to monetary theory. In general, I have used little documentation in this book. Readers interested in the sources of, and justifications for, statements made here—particularly statements of what studies show—will find them set out in my *Monetary Policy in the United States* (New York: Random House, in preparation). That book develops in greater detail a number of the topics touched on lightly here.

In conclusion, I would like to express my gratitude for helpful comments in particular to Professor Harlan Smith, the editor of this series, and to Thomas Cargill, John Culbertson, Milton Friedman, David Laidler, Charles Schotta, W. P. Strassmann, Richard Thorn, and Clark Warburton —none of whom are, of course, responsible for any remaining errors. I am also indebted to Mr. Theodore Caris of Random House, to Mrs. Dolores Byrne, who typed the manuscript, and to Miss Susan Sperling, of Random House, for her excellent editorial work.

Davis, California   **Thomas Mayer**
November, 1967

Contents

ELEMENTS OF
MONETARY POLICY

Chapter 1 | The Goals of Monetary Policy

Monetary policy has four major goals. They are full employment, price stability, economic growth, and balance-of-payments equilibrium. Table 1 shows the extent to which the United States has met these goals in recent years. There is widespread agreement about the desirability of these goals, but they are only vaguely defined in the general consensus and stand partly in a competitive relationship to each other. So let us look at them in greater detail.

Full employment is, of course, entirely consistent with some frictional unemployment, that is, an unemployment rate of 3 or 4 percent as measured by our statistical series. Whether the target should be a 3 percent rate, a 4 percent rate, or a 5 percent rate is a matter of dispute, with conservatives generally advocating a higher rate than liberals.

Price stability is also not a straightforward idea. To be realistic, price stability must be interpreted as consistent with some, quite minor, price change but should this change be ¼ percent a year, or can it be as high as 1 percent, or even perhaps 2 percent? This problem is complicated by the fact that the Consumer Price Index appears to have an upward bias. New

TABLE 1 *Selected Economic Indicators 1947–1966*

Year	GNP in 1958 Prices	Unemployment Rate	Labor Force Time Lost Through Unemployment and Part Time Employment[a]	Consumers Price Index (1957–1959 = 100)	Wholesale Price Index (1957–1959 = 100)	GNP Price Index (1958 = 100)	Surplus or Deficit in the Balance of Payments[b] (Billions of Dollars)	United States Gold Stock Plus Foreign Currency Holdings[c] (Billions of Dollars)
1948	323.7	3.8%	—	83.8	87.9	79.6	0.8	24.4
1949	324.1	5.9	—	83.0	83.5	79.1	0.1	24.6
1950	355.3	5.3	—	83.8	86.8	80.2	− 3.5	22.8
1951	383.4	3.3	—	90.5	96.7	85.6	− 0.8	22.9
1952	395.1	3.1	—	92.5	94.0	87.5	− 1.2	23.3
1953	412.8	2.9	—	93.2	92.7	88.3	− 2.2	22.1
1954	407.0	5.6	—	93.6	92.9	89.6	− 1.5	21.8
1955	438.0	4.4	5.1%[d]	93.3	93.2	90.9	− 1.2	21.8
1956	446.1	4.2		94.7	96.2	94.0	− 1.0	22.1

1957	452.5	4.3	5.3	98.0	99.0	97.5	0.6	22.9
1958	447.3	6.8	8.1	100.7	100.4	100.0	− 3.4	20.6
1959	475.9	5.5	6.6	101.5	100.6	101.6	− 3.9	19.5
1960	487.7	5.6	6.7	103.1	100.7	103.3	− 3.9	17.8
1961	497.2	6.7	8.0	104.2	100.3	104.6	− 2.4	17.1
1962	529.8	5.6	6.7	105.4	100.6	105.8	− 2.2	16.2
1963	551.0	5.7	6.4	106.7	100.3	107.2	− 2.7	15.8
1964	580.0	5.2	5.8	108.1	100.5	108.9	− 2.8	15.9
1965	614.4	4.6	5.0	109.9	102.5	110.9	− 1.3	14.6
1966	647.7ᵖ	3.9	4.2	113.1	105.8ᵖ	114.2ᵖ	− 1.2ᵉ	14.6ᵖ

ᵖ Denotes preliminary

ᵃ Beginning 1963 this series not strictly comparable with preceding data

ᵇ Liquidity basis

ᶜ Convertible foreign currencies held by United States monetary authorities only

ᵈ Data not available prior to 1956

ᵉ Average for first three quarters at seasonally adjusted rates

SOURCE: *Economic Report of the President* (Washington, D.C., 1967), pp. 214, 216, 239, 262, 264, 307, and 312.

commodities are included in the index only after they have come into fairly common use so that the index does not catch the price decline that usually occurs as a commodity evolves from a specialty item into a generally used one. Moreover, the index does not give sufficient weight to quality improvements. An obvious example is medical services. Suppose that a physician's fee rises from $5 to $10 a visit but that illnesses formerly requiring three visits to clear up can now be cured in one visit. Has the price of medical services gone down or up? The Consumer Price Index treats such a situation as a price increase. In view of this bias in the index, should one define price stability as an annual increase by 1 or 2 percent in the Consumer Price Index rather than as a constant index?

Another problem is whether the price level should be measured by the Consumer Price Index, by the Wholesale Price Index, or by the GNP deflator.[1] This question can have important policy implications. Thus, in the period 1960 to 1964 the Consumer Price Index rose by 4.8 percent, while the Wholesale Price Index declined slightly. In these years, should the Federal Reserve have been worrying about inflation or rejoicing in price stability?

Economic growth involves the problem of deciding what rate of growth is sustainable. Federal Reserve officials have suggested that the growth rate may be increased at certain times in the *short run* by infla-

[1] The Consumer Price Index has the advantage of tying in better with the nation's ultimate economic well-being than does the Wholesale Price Index. But, on the other hand, the consumer index is sluggish and signals price changes much more slowly than the wholesale index; and in addition, the quality change problem is more severe for the consumer index than for the wholesale index. The GNP deflator is largely a mixture of the Consumer Price Index and the Wholesale Price Index (though it does include government services too) and hence has some of the characteristics of both.

tionary policies but that such growth would not be sustainable in the long run and that monetary policy should aim at sustainable growth. But the concept of sustainable growth is imprecise.

Finally, balance-of-payments equilibrium is also not a clear-cut idea. To start with, different methods of measuring the balance of payments give different results, and, in addition, it is not at all clear whether balance-of-payments *equilibrium* is consistent with a small *deficit* in the balance of payments. The dollar is used as a reserve currency by many countries, and since the demand for international reserves grows over time, some deficit in the United States balance of payments may be consistent with balance-of-payments equilibrium. Clearly, the size of such an "equilibrium deficit" and even its very existence is a matter of judgment.

The vagueness of these goals means that the success of a stabilization policy is sometimes a matter of dispute.

These four goals, stated at the beginning of this chapter—full employment, price stability, economic growth, and balance-of-payments equilibrium—are not the only goals pursued by United States monetary policy. During World War I, the overriding aim was to facilitate the sale of government securities, while during World War II and until 1951 the dominant aim was to maintain stable prices for government securities. Another goal is the maintenance of the private enterprise system in that the Federal Reserve has tried to limit the extent to which monetary policy interferes with the free market. Moreover, a major aim of Federal Reserve policy has been to ensure the soundness of the banking system by limiting the occurrence of money market conditions which would tempt banks to make unsound loans. While this aim can, in principle, be treated as merely a *means* to goals discussed above, the Federal Reserve has given it so much emphasis that, at least at times, it has almost appeared to be an independent goal. Thus, in 1929 the Federal Reserve was so eager to limit speculation that it disavowed any concern with "the larger public consequences" of its action to limit speculation.

If one accepts the Federal Reserve's current goals in broad general terms, there remains a serious problem of the multiplicity of goals. There is a serious question whether or not all of these goals are compatible. The general feeling of the Federal Reserve is that they *are* compatible, and, indeed, that they are interrelated. In this view, price stability (or perhaps a slowly declining price level) is necessary to maintain full employment and economic growth. While inflation might help to raise employment and the growth rate in the short run, an inflationary boom leads to maladjustments that make the subsequent recession much more severe. Conversely, sharply falling prices are bad for employment, so that price stability (or perhaps gently falling prices) and full employment make up a single package rather than competing goals. Similarly, price stability and balance-of-payments equilibrium are compatible because America can achieve balance-of-payments equilibrium only if the domestic price level is kept under control so that our country does not price itself out of foreign markets. The Federal Reserve sees little conflict arising from its many goals. Such a feeling that various policy goals are compatible is a common and natural one among government officials. A belief that goals are *not* compatible would require an official to choose among them and to support policies that hinder the achievement of one or more of our national goals. Obviously, the people who have to make the hard decisions, unlike those who merely write books about them, tend to play down the conflict among goals. This statement should not be interpreted as a denial that there is *some* complementarity among the various goals—for example, a wild speculative boom probably *does* make the ensuing recession worse by resulting in excessive investment and other maladjustments. But although there is some degree of complementarity, there is also some potential for conflict.

Full employment and price level stability may conflict in several ways. For example, if there is so-called "cost-push" inflation, that is, inflation initiated by sellers of either labor or products pushing up their prices, curbing this kind of inflation may necessitate creating so much unemployment and excess capacity that sellers cease to demand higher prices. There is a large literature about the relation between wage changes and unemployment (the so-called "Phillips curve") that suggests that substantial unemployment would be needed to keep wages rising no faster than productivity.

Another, and perhaps more relevant, way in which full employment and price level stability may be incompatible is the following. Stabilization policies take some time to become effective, and since our forecasting ability is still fairly limited, a policy of ensuring that aggregate demand will be sufficient for full employment sometimes results in aggregate demand being excessive, and, hence, inflationary. (Conversely, a policy of controlling aggregate demand so that it is never inflationary is likely to lead at times to a deficiency in demand.) A firm commitment to full employment therefore tends to be inflationary. Hence, it *may* be inflation rather than price stability that is compatible with full employment. Even in the long run it is quite doubtful that moderate inflation is bad for employment. In the postwar period we have had a moderate secular inflation, at least as measured by our price indexes, and it has not resulted in maladjustments leading to a severe depression.

Similarly, so far at least, there is little evidence that price stability is necessary for rapid economic growth. Looking at growth rates and price trends in various countries in the postwar period, one sees little correlation between the two. While this lack of correlation is not firm evidence, it suggests that moderate inflation does not hurt the growth rate.

Price stability and balance-of-payments equilibrium, too, are not necessarily related. Granted that inflation tends to worsen the balance of payments, it is not at all clear that price *stability* is consistent with balance-of-payments equilibrium. If foreign prices are rising, balance-of-payments equilibrium may require rising prices in the United States to prevent a recurrence of a dollar shortage. On the other hand, if world demand shifts away from United States products and assets, or if the United States develops a greater taste for imports or for foreign assets, then balance-of-payments equilibrium requires a *decline* in the domestic price level. Given changes in world trade patterns and in foreign prices, it would be a coincidence if balance-of-payments considerations would call for a stable price level.[2]

The other two goals, full employment and rapid growth, may also be inconsistent with balance-of-payments equilibrium since both full employment and rapid growth are likely to lead to an increase in imports. To be sure, rapid growth *may* also spur ex-

[2] This assumes stable exchange rates and no changes in trade barriers. The balance-of-payments problem is discussed in detail in Delbert Snider, *International Monetary Relations* (New York: Random House, 1966).

ports and, in addition, may make domestic investment so profitable that an improvement in the capital account offsets, or more than offsets, the deterioration of the current account. But there is no assurance that this would actually happen.

Given this possible clash of goals, what should the Federal Reserve do? It does not have enough tools to aim at all of its goals simultaneously, even if they were not mutually conflicting. But as long as the Federal Reserve is officially committed to multiple goals, it must claim that any action it takes to achieve any one of them does not conflict with the achievement of another one. This puts the Federal Reserve under great pressure to be at times vague and obscure in its statements and thinking. This problem could be solved by requiring monetary policy to concentrate on only one goal. The one usually suggested is price level stability. Concentrating on this single goal can be defended in several ways. One contends that all the goals are interrelated so that while stabilizing the price level would not necessarily guarantee full employment and balance-of-payments equilibrium, it would go a long way toward meeting these goals. For example, if businessmen have the assurance of price stability, they are less likely to cut back investment during a recession than if they expect prices to fall. Opinions vary on the extent to which price stability would help in preventing fluctuations in output. Economists who accept a monetary theory of the cycle or one that stresses maladjustments tend to give more weight to price stability as a curative factor than those economists who accept a more Keynesian explanation like the multiplier-accelerator mechanism.

Since monetary policy is not capable of achieving all the above goals fully, let it be confined to the more feasible task of meeting one of them directly and for the other goals rely on the favorable by-products of meeting the one goal.

A second approach is to say that monetary policy is not the only stabilization tool but is supplemented by fiscal policy. If monetary policy is directed towards maintaining price stability, fiscal policy can be left to deal with the employment problem.[3] Another possibility is to use fiscal policy to achieve the domestic goals and confine monetary policy to dealing with the balance-of-payments problem. Since monetary policy has a *comparative* advantage over fiscal policy in handling a balance-of-payments disequilibrium, such a division of labor has much to recommend it. But given the difficulties of using fiscal policy successfully for domestic stabilization, monetary policy (rightly or wrongly) is used for this task too.

Note that this is a comparative and not necessarily an absolute advantage. The reason monetary policy has this comparative advantage is that it affects the balance of payments in two ways. Like fiscal policy it affects the current account by changing the level of income and, hence, imports and exports. In addition, by changing interest rates monetary policy has some effect on the capital account of the balance of pay-

[3] Monetary policy is quite distinct from fiscal policy. Monetary policy concerns the amount of money available, while fiscal policy involves taxation and government expenditures. This proposed division of labor creates two problems, however. First, it still leaves two goals untended: economic growth and balance-of-payments equilibrium. (It is *not* correct to say that flexible exchange rates unaided by monetary policy could take care of the balance-of-payments problem—see Robert Mundell, "Problems of Monetary and Exchange Rate Management in Canada," *National Banking Review*, Vol. 2, No. 1 [September, 1964], pp. 77–86.) Second, since output and the price level are connected (which is, after all, what a stable aggregate supply curve implies), an attempt to handle them separately would fail if full employment and price stability should turn out to be incompatible.

ments. (To be sure, fiscal policy also has some indirect effects on interest rates since these are influenced by the level of income. But clearly monetary policy has more control over interest rates than does fiscal policy.) In fact, it can be shown that the opposite policy of using fiscal policy to cure a balance-of-payments disequilibrium and monetary policy to achieve the domestic goals leads to instability.[4]

Confining monetary policy to a single goal provides a yardstick for evaluating the performance of the money managers. As long as monetary policy does *not* have a single goal, anyone attempting to evaluate the record of monetary policy faces an exasperating task, as exemplified by the following comment of Senator William Proxmire to Chairman William McChesney Martin at a Congressional hearing:

> I have the greatest respect for your ability, and I think that you are an outstanding and competent person, and everybody agrees with that, but the fact is, that when you try to come down and discuss this in meaningful specific terms, it is like nailing a custard pie to the wall. . . . And frankly, Mr. Martin, without specific goals, criteria, guidelines, it is impossible to exercise any congressional oversight over you, and I think you know it.[5]

The Federal Reserve has not accepted the view that it should confine itself to a single goal. Instead, it has stressed the interrelatedness of all four goals and, hence, the need to look at the behavior of the whole economy rather than at any single index in isolation. Moreover, the Federal Reserve believes that since many factors not under its control influence the price

[4] See Robert Mundell, "The Appropriate Use of Monetary and Fiscal Policy for Internal and External Stability," *Staff Papers,* Vol. 9 (March, 1962), pp. 70–77.
[5] Cited in John Culbertson, *Full Employment or Stagnation?* (New York: McGraw-Hill, 1964), pp. 15–55.

level, it cannot pledge itself to keep the price index or any other index stable.

Given the fact that the Federal Reserve aims at several goals at the same time, can one say that it gives more emphasis to one goal than to another? This important question deserves a straightforward answer, if possible. Unfortunately, several difficulties make it impossible. First, a statement that the Federal Reserve prefers, say, price stability to full employment is meaningless unless one first specifies the quantities involved. For example, in all probability, the Federal Reserve prefers a 1 percent price increase a year to stable prices accompanied by continuous unemployment of 10 percent, while, at the same time, preferring a 3 percent unemployment rate with stable prices to a situation where unemployment is only 2 percent but prices are rising at an annual rate of 20 percent. To say whether the Federal Reserve prefers one goal to another one must specify the "trade-off" between the two.[6] Note, moreover, that this trade-off is not constant but changes as the *levels* of the variables change. A rise in unemployment by one percentage point gives rise to less concern if it means a rise from 2 percent to 3 percent than if it means a rise from 5 percent to 6 percent. The problem is further complicated by the fact that Federal Reserve officials never state explicitly what they consider the proper trade-off to be.

It is, therefore, *not* possible to give a straightforward answer to the question posed above. However, it is possible to give a roundabout answer, by comparing the Federal Reserve's trade-off with that of, say, the Council of Economic Advisers in recent years. It appears that the Federal Reserve attaches *relatively* more

---

[6] This is simply a manifestation of the fact that you generally cannot tell if someone prefers commodity A to commodity B unless you know the quantities of A and B being offered.

importance to price stability and relatively less importance to full employment than does the Council of Economic Advisers. Similarly, the Federal Reserve seems to be more concerned with balance-of-payments equilibrium and less concerned with economic growth than is the Council of Economic Advisers.[7] Note, however, two qualifications to these statements: First, they are not based on any hard and fast evidence, but are merely the general impressions of some economists. Second, these statements do not, by any means, imply that the Federal Reserve is not interested in full employment and economic growth or that the Council of Economic Advisors does not value price stability and balance-of-payments equilibrium—their concern is merely a matter of degree. Various interest groups have their spokesmen in the government—the farmers have the Department of Agriculture, business has the Department of Commerce, and labor the Department of Labor. To some extent the Federal Reserve seems to look upon itself as the only spokesman for creditors and other fixed income groups who are hurt by inflation.

This choice of relative priorities has resulted in a great deal of criticism of the Federal Reserve, perhaps more than of any other aspect of its policy. Consider, for example, the following recent episode. In the period of 1958 to 1962 unemployment rates were high (varying from 6.8 percent in 1958 to 5.5 percent in 1959), and the rate of economic growth was disappointing. The cumulative gap between potential and actual output during this period was $170 billion (in 1962 prices) so that even if one makes some allowance for the fact that a full employment policy could not

---

[7] This statement refers to the average attitude of recent Councils and therefore reflects the results of recent elections. Future election results may change the picture.

achieve full potential output the failure to adopt expansionary policies cost the nation $25 billion per year
in this period.[8] But since the Consumer Price Index
rose from 100.7 in 1958 to 105.4 in 1962 and there was
a balance-of-payments deficit, the Federal Reserve
adopted a tight money policy in spite of high unemployment. While the money supply had been allowed
to grow at an annual rate of just over 2 percent from
1948 to 1958, it grew on an average only ½ percent
from mid-1959 to mid-1962. Monetary policy has therefore been blamed for initiating the 1960 recession as
well as for the very slow recovery.[9] Similarly, the
Federal Reserve has been blamed for other recessions,
for example, the 1937 downturn.

The goals so far discussed are high-level goals—
they relate to the ultimate ends of monetary policy.
But the Federal Reserve needs proximate goals, too.
The Federal Open Market Committee cannot just tell
the account manager in New York to maintain full
employment. The Federal Reserve's high-level goals
have to be translated into specific operating instruc-
tions.

Within the money market, the Federal Reserve has
a series of intermediate goals. They include the stock
of money, the long-term interest rate, the total credit
supply, and the supply of bank credit. It is by changing these variables that the Federal Reserve attempts

---

[8] Culbertson, *op. cit.*, p. 22.

[9] *Ibid.*, pp. 123–128. Culbertson attributes the Federal Reserve's
tight money policy not only to a deemphasis of full employment relative to price stability, but also to its emphasis on
credit conditions—a point discussed below. The best defense
of the restrictive policy is that velocity was rising in these
years, hence only a small increase in the money stock was
"needed." But the critics of the Federal Reserve respond that
the reason velocity was rising was that the restrictive monetary
policy had raised interest rates. And this increase in interest
rates reduced investment.

to bring about changes in income. But even these variables are some distance removed from the Federal Reserve's direct control point—the volume of bank reserves. The Federal Reserve, therefore, conducts its operations with the help of a series of money market guides that it hopes will help it reach its money market goals. Among these money market guides are the total reserve base, "free reserves" (i.e., total reserves minus both required reserves and borrowings from the Federal Reserve), member bank borrowing, the Federal Funds rate and the Treasury bills rate, the Federal Reserve's "feel" of the money market, and so forth. These are variables the Federal Reserve feels are closely under its control and, hence, provide convenient guides. For example, if the Federal Reserve wants to increase the money stock, it decides that the volume of bank reserves must increase and, hence, it undertakes open market operations (discussed in the next chapter) to raise the reserve base.

These money market techniques of the Federal Reserve have come in for a great deal of criticism in recent years.[10] One point the critics have raised is that by not making a forthright decision among the various money market goals (the money stock, interest rates, etc.), the Federal Reserve is not following a policy that has a clear-cut and tested theory behind it. Another point is that the money market guides the Federal Reserve uses are not closely linked to its money market goals so that if the Federal Reserve follows these guides, it may not be able to reach its money market goals. One dramatic illustration of this problem is that in much of the postwar period the money

[10] The issues raised by this debate are quite complex and can only be hinted at here. For a more detailed discussion see my *Monetary Policy in the United States* (New York: Random House, in preparation), Chapter 3.

stock has risen at a faster rate during an expansion than during a recession; that is, it has acted procyclically. To be sure, this behavior is found only if the money supply is defined as currency and demand deposits and not if time deposits are included and, moreover, the money stock is only one of several Federal Reserve goals. However, this behavior of the money supply does raise some questions about whether the Federal Reserve's policy has been countercyclical rather than procyclical.

In concluding this first chapter, a brief outline of what is to come would be helpful. Chapter 2 discusses the tools of monetary policy: the ways in which the Federal Reserve changes bank reserves. Chapter 3 carries the story forward by looking at the resulting effects on expenditures. Chapter 4 describes the resource allocation effects of monetary policy and raises the question whether or not monetary policy is fast enough in its effects to be a useful stabilization tool. The final chapter pulls this material together by comparing different monetary policies.

Chapter **2** | **The Tools
of Monetary
Policy**

The previous chapter discussed the goals of monetary policy. This chapter deals with the tools the Federal Reserve uses to reach these goals. There are three major domestic tools: open-market operations, the discount mechanism, and reserve-requirement changes. After discussing each of these major tools in the order given, the chapter takes up their interrelations and their relative advantages and disadvantages. This material is followed by a discussion of the five minor domestic tools: selective controls, moral suasion, direct action, publicity, and informal advice. A brief concluding section deals with international tools.

The Federal Reserve is not the only institution possessing tools of monetary policy. The Treasury too has some monetary powers; for example, it can change bank reserves by shifting its cash holdings between commercial banks and the Federal Reserve and has occasionally done so to give the Federal Reserve's policy a small assist. Much more significant is the Treasury's control over financial conditions through its debt management policies. Since debt management belongs as much in the area of fiscal policy as of monetary policy it is relegated to an Appendix of this chapter. Government lending agencies, too, have some monetary powers as do the FDIC and FSLIC, which can affect the relative size of deposits in banks and nonbank institutions through their regulations.[1]

Mechanics of Open-Market Operations

Open-market operations are now the most important tool of monetary policy despite the fact that they were not even recognized as a tool in the Federal Reserve's early history. The original Federal Reserve Act (1913) envisaged that the Federal Reserve Banks would hold government securities to obtain earnings and would from time to time buy and sell these securities to maximize their earnings. The Federal Reserve Banks soon realized, however, that by buying and selling securities they were changing bank reserves. Accordingly, starting in 1922 the Federal Reserve Banks decided to coordinate their purchases and sales. From this modest beginning evolved the modern, highly centralized, organization of open-market operations.

Decisions to undertake open-market operations are made by the Federal Open Market Committee (officially, the seven members of the Board of Governors and five presidents of the Federal Reserve Banks, though actually the presidents of other Federal Reserve Banks usually attend the sessions but do not vote). This Committee usually meets every three weeks and its decisions are communicated to the "Trading Desk" of the Federal Reserve Bank of New York, which carries out the transactions. The Com-

[1] The Federal Reserve can, and has, put pressure on the banking system by not allowing banks to pay a sufficiently high rate on time deposits to compete with open-market instruments. It is too early to tell whether or not such pressure will become a regular tool of monetary policy.

mittee's decisions are stated in fairly broad terms; for example, it might say to allow for only a small growth of the reserve base and to keep the money market under moderate pressure. Purchases and sales are undertaken in New York, the main money market of the country. All Federal Reserve Banks have a prorata share in the securities bought or sold.

The Federal Reserve Bank of New York deals with a handful of specialized firms that make up a market in government securities, the so-called primary dealers. The Trading Desk of the New York bank is in constant touch with them, continually asking for bids and offers to sell, thus feeling out the money market. From these and other contacts in the market the New York bank acquires a detailed knowledge of the market and prides itself on having the "feel of the market," to use a favorite Federal Reserve phrase. It is therefore able to adjust its purchases and sales to continually changing conditions. Note that nobody is forced to buy from or sell to the Federal Reserve. Government securities are sold in an over-the-counter market, and the Federal Reserve buys or sells at the prices quoted by the dealers.

The securities in which the Federal Reserve deals are federal government securities, primarily short-term securities. The Federal Reserve has the legal power to deal in a fairly wide variety of instruments: eligible bills of exchange, bankers acceptances, government securities, direct or fully guaranteed securities of government agencies, certain state and local securities, and foreign exchange. Most transactions are in Treasury bills, the shortest term securities issued. If the Federal Reserve undertakes open-market purchases that it intends to reverse later, it may let the market know this by using so-called "repurchase agreements." Under this arrangement, the Federal Reserve buys securities from dealers who commit themselves to repurchase these securities at a certain date, usually at a fixed price. This arrangement is neither a loan to the dealers nor an outright open-market purchase but lies somewhere between the two. One of the uses of the repurchase agreements is to provide dealers with temporary funds at a time of a Treasury financing or during some other temporary stringency in the money market. Sometimes the Federal Reserve undertakes "reverse" repurchase agreements selling securities to dealers with a commitment to buy them back.

Effects of Open-Market Operations

Today open-market operations constitute the main way of changing bank reserves. If the Federal Reserve buys securities from a member bank (or a nonmember bank having an account with it), it credits the proceeds to the bank's reserve account, and bank reserves are increased directly. Conversely, if the Federal Reserve sells securities to a member bank, it debits the bank's account.

The same effects occur if the Federal Reserve deals with a nonbank (i.e., anyone except a bank). If the Federal Reserve buys securities, it issues a check to the seller, and the seller deposits it in his bank. The bank then sends it to the Federal Reserve for clearing, and the Federal Reserve credits the bank's account. Conversely, if the Federal Reserve sells securities to nonbanks, the seller draws a check on his bank, and the Federal Reserve debits the bank's account. The only difference is that if the Federal Reserve deals with a nonbank, bank deposits are directly affected by the open-market operations, whereas if the Federal Reserve deals with a bank only bank reserves are directly affected. But unless banks decide to change their volume of excess reserves this makes no difference.

Expressed in the language of "T accounts," the sale of securities by the Federal Reserve to a member bank has the following effects:

Federal Reserve System		Commercial Bank	
Assets	*Liabilities*	*Assets*	*Liabilities*
Securities held —	Member bank reserves —	Deposits with Federal Reserve — Securities held +	

If a nonbank had bought these securities from the Federal Reserve, the Federal Reserve account would look the same way, but the commercial bank's account would change as follows:

Assets	*Liabilities*
Deposits with the Federal Reserve —	Demand deposits —

In addition to having this effect on the reserve base, open-market operations also affect the economy through their effect on expectations. Money market analysts watch the weekly balance sheet of the New York Federal Reserve Bank and try to see if open-market operations indicate any changes in monetary policy. This "announcement effect" of Federal Reserve action is less for open-market operations than for rediscount rate changes and therefore is not discussed here, but in the following section.

Open-market operations are used by the Federal Reserve for both so-called "defensive" and "dynamic" operations. Such factors as Treasury gold purchases, changes in float, changes in currency in circulation, and so forth continually impinge on the reserve base. The Federal Reserve Bank of New York goes to substantial trouble to forecast these "market factors" and then to offset them by open-market operations if these factors threaten to change the reserve base in an undesired direction or by an undesired amount. These activities are called "defensive operations" since the Federal Reserve is merely defending the reserve base against factors tending to change it.

On the other hand, Federal Reserve open-market operations to *change* the reserve base are called "dynamic operations." Unfortunately, it is not always easy to distinguish between the two for two major reasons: First, assume, for example, that bank reserves have increased in a certain week and that the balance sheet of the New York Federal Reserve Bank has shown security purchases. This does not necessarily mean that the Federal Reserve adopted a dynamic policy to raise bank reserves. In undertaking defensive operations the Federal Reserve acts on the basis of *estimates* of the changes in reserves resulting from market factors. These estimates may be in error. Thus, in a particular week when reserves have increased the Federal Reserve may not have intended this to happen; it may have bought securities merely to offset an expected reserve drain that did not materialize.

The second difficulty is that changes in monetary policy are usually not abrupt. Often they occur in frequent, but almost imperceptibly small, steps. In the beginning, the Federal Reserve may merely tend in its forecast of market factors to lean more towards one side, for example, caution, than towards the other, expansion.[2] This makes it hard to distinguish between

[2] Estimates of changes in reserves necessarily give a range, but there is no reason why the Federal Reserve should use the mean of this range or even the most probable value as the best figure for action. After all, a driver who thinks he has a 51 percent chance of passing a car without an accident, i.e., whose "best" estimate is that he *can* pass, will usually not try to do so.

defensive and dynamic operations since policies in these areas are intertwined.[3]

Defensive operations account for a large part of total open-market operations. For example, in the six months of April through September, 1961, the Federal Reserve undertook total open-market operations (adding purchases and sales) of $10.5 billion, but purchases and sales largely cancelled each other so that the net addition to reserves was only $0.7 billion.[4] This great amount of market churning has been criticized as unnecessary. If the Federal Reserve would lengthen the reserve settlement period of member banks (i.e., the period over which the reserves of banks are averaged and compared to required reserves) to one month and, further, if it would stagger the reserve settlements so that they occur on different days for different banks, market factors affecting reserves would largely cancel out. Large-scale defensive operations would then not be required.[5]

Advantages and Disadvantages of Open-Market Operations

Open-market operations are the best weapon of the Federal Reserve for both defensive and dynamic operations for several reasons. First, the Federal Reserve can buy or sell enough government securities to make the reserve base anything it pleases; there is more

[3] For a masterly example of the detective work necessary to separate intended from unintended reserve changes, see Hobart Carr, "Why and How to Read the Federal Reserve Statement," *Journal of Finance*, Vol. 14 (December, 1959), pp. 504–519.

[4] Albert Cox, Jr. and Ralph Leach, "Defensive Open Market Operations and the Reserve Settlement Periods of Member Banks," *Journal of Finance*, Vol. 19 (March, 1964), p. 79.

[5] *Ibid.*, pp. 76–93. For a defense of the present arrangement, see Peter Sternlight, "Reserve Settlement Periods of Member Banks: Comment," *Journal of Finance*, Vol. 19 (March, 1964), pp. 94–98.

than enough ammunition. Second, open-market operations occur at the initiative of the Federal Reserve, unlike the case of discount rate changes where the Federal Reserve can only encourage or discourage banks to borrow but has no direct control of the volume involved. Third, open-market operations can be carried out in small steps, very small steps if need be. This gradual pace allows the Federal Reserve to make quite precise adjustments in the reserve base. This ability to make small changes is, of course, most useful for defensive operations where the Federal Reserve may want to offset market factors causing minor changes in reserves.

Fourth, open-market operations can be used continually. This allows the Federal Reserve to adjust the reserve base on a continuous basis as it receives new information about the impact of market factors on reserves and as its "feel of the market" changes. Given this ability to move rapidly and in large or small steps the Federal Reserve really does have fingertip control over the reserve base.

Fifth and finally, the open-market operations can be reversed easily. The Federal Reserve can buy at 10 A.M. and sell at 11 A.M., and since the Trading Desk's assessment of money-market conditions is continually subject to revision, this ability to reverse the field is highly prized by the Federal Reserve. None of the other tools are so easily reversible. If the Federal Reserve were to change the discount rate continually, it might give the impression of not knowing what it wants to do. With open-market operations, however, actions that are reversed within the statement week do not come to the public's attention.

To be sure, open-market operations do suffer from one disadvantage. Their initial impact is concentrated in New York, and there is some evidence that it takes some time for their impact to be felt fully throughout the country.

The Discount Mechanism

Federal Reserve member banks can replenish their reserves by borrowing from the Federal Reserve Bank of their district if they meet certain not very restrictive conditions. (In principle, the Federal Reserve can lend to nonmember banks as well as to anyone else, but this provision of the law exists to take care of the special conditions of a financial panic, rather than for ordinary borrowing.)

Originally, member banks borrowed by *re*discounting the commercial paper (i.e., promissory notes) that they themselves had discounted for their customers. The Federal Reserve Banks imposed strict regulations on the type of paper they were willing to discount or rediscount, as it is sometimes called. It had to be short-term paper arising from self-liquidating commercial operations.[6] Commercial paper that showed that the customer had used the proceeds for such financial transactions as purchases of common stock were not eligible for rediscounting. By limiting its discounting to a special type of paper called *eligible* paper, the Federal Reserve tried to control the *quality* of credit. This was in accordance with the real-bills doctrine

[6] Self-liquidating loans are loans used to finance transactions which *in themselves* generate the funds necessary to repay them. For example, a loan used by a merchant to acquire inventory is said to be self-liquidating since the sale of the inventory in the normal course of business provides the merchant with funds to repay the loan. Similarly, loans to merchants to pay wages are considered self-liquidating. By contrast, neither a consumer loan or a mortgage loan is self-liquidating. Although the customer is able to repay the loan, he does not do so out of funds generated by the loan itself.

(commercial credit theory) which had substantial support at that time.[7]

But for many years now banks have not actually discounted their customer's paper; instead they have borrowed usually on their own promissory notes backed by government securities. Banks can, and very occasionally do, use eligible paper to secure their borrowing, but for technical reasons it is more convenient for banks to use government securities. But the use of eligible paper to secure borrowing may be in for a modest revival. Since banks have to secure government deposits (Federal, state, and local) by pledging government securities, a number of banks are running short of unpledged government securities needed as security when they borrow from the Federal Reserve on their own notes.

Another change has been the abandonment of the real-bills doctrine as a criterion for discounting. This does not mean that banks are allowed to borrow an unlimited amount—for any purpose. Banks are supposed to borrow only for short-term reserve adjustments. Borrowing should be for "need," and not for profit, that is, they are not supposed to borrow merely because the Treasury bill rate is above the discount rate so that they can make a profit by borrowing and buying Treasury bills with the proceeds.[8] Whether or

[7] The real-bills doctrine, or commercial loan theory as it is sometimes called, is a theory which asserts that banks should make only short-term self-liquidating loans. This view, now generally considered fallacious, had wide acceptance when the Federal Reserve was organized. Hence, to give banks an incentive to make short-term and self-liquidating loans, only commercial paper that met these criteria was "acceptable paper" for rediscounting.

[8] The distinction between borrowing for need and borrowing for profit is quite hazy at times. To be sure, if a bank borrows and then buys securities or makes loans it can be said to borrow for profit rather than for need. But how about a bank

not banks actually do borrow for need and not for profit is a controversial issue.

In principle, though perhaps less in practice, borrowing is considered by the Federal Reserve to be a privilege of membership and not a right. The Federal Reserve feels that its funds belong to all the member banks and that it would be improper to allow any bank to make "undue" use of these collective funds to gain an unfair competitive advantage over other banks. To be sure, the Federal Reserve generally does not refuse a loan to a bank since a refusal might endanger the bank, but as a Federal Reserve official put it, "We help a bank decide not to borrow from us." [9]

Another limitation on borrowing from the Federal Reserve arises out of banking tradition and policy. American banks have a tradition against borrowing, a tradition at least in part explained by the disastrous effects of borrowing that showed up in nineteenth-century financial panics. Many banks are proud of the fact that they never borrow from the Federal Reserve. During a "fairly active year" about 20 percent of the member banks borrow at one time or another, and at any one time about 10 percent are currently indebted.[10] When a bank does borrow it is under pressure to repay rapidly. The Federal Reserve, therefore, feels that a dollar of borrowed reserves is less expansionary than a dollar of owned reserves.

---

that borrows to meet a deposit drain that it could also have met by selling securities? Is it borrowing for need or profit? Similarly, suppose that a bank operates on a very thin margin of excess reserves and therefore has to borrow frequently as unexpected deposit drains occur. Is it borrowing for need or profit? By and large, the term "need" has little place in economic analysis.

[9] Robert Roosa quoted in Charles Whittlesey, "Credit Policy at the Discount Window," *Quarterly Journal of Economics*, Vol. 73 (May, 1959), p. 211.

[10] *Ibid.*, p. 212.

Still another limitation on borrowing relates to the use made of the borrowed funds. The Federal Reserve has a traditional distaste for speculation, and banks are not supposed to borrow if they are at the same time making an unduly large volume of loans to speculators. This regulation is limited in its effectiveness because a man may borrow from his bank for regular business purposes and then use for speculation his own funds that he otherwise would have spent for these business purposes.

The discount rate that the Federal Reserve charges is usually kept fairly close to the Treasury bill rate, though it often lags behind at turns.[11] But since the discount rate is changed fairly infrequently, the two rates do tend to get out of line.

Changes in the Discount Rate

Changes in the discount rate were originally the only major tool of monetary policy. This was copied by the framers of the Federal Reserve Act from the British system, where the Bank of England relied on changes in its "bank rate" to control the money market.

But already in the early 1920's the discount rate mechanism was supplemented by the development of open-market operations as a credit control tool. For some years after 1933, bank reserves were greatly in excess of legal requirements, and very little borrowing from the Federal Reserve took place. The discount mechanism seemed unimportant, and in the nineteen years of 1934 through 1952 the New York Federal Reserve Bank changed its discount rate only eight times.

[11] The Treasury bill rate is usually treated as the rate that is competitive with the rediscount rate because Treasury bills (the shortest term government securities) have a highly organized market and are extremely liquid.

Since then, money has become tighter, banks have had more incentive to borrow, and the Federal Reserve has put much more emphasis on the discount rate and has changed it much more frequently.

In the Federal Reserve's view, changes in the discount rate act to control the money stock and credit extension in two ways. First, there is the cost effect. Raising the discount rate makes borrowing more expensive and, hence, reduces the volume of borrowing, while, conversely, lowering the rediscount rate encourages banks to borrow.

Second, there is a more complex effect of expectations usually called the "announcement effect." Changes in the discount rate are dramatic—unlike open-market operations, they frequently make the front page of newspapers. Hence, even if it should turn out that the *cost* effect of the rate increase on bank borrowing is minor, the rise in the rate serves notice on the financial community that the Federal Reserve is likely to use its other, more powerful tools soon. Thus, if the discount rate is raised, the public's expectations may be changed. Borrowers, the Federal Reserve asserts, will reevaluate their investment plans when they realize that interest rates are rising. At the same time, lenders will be less willing to lend because they expect interest rates to rise even further. Thus, a rise in the discount rate reduces *both* the supply and demand for loans and, hence, reduces investment.

Moreover, even firms not currently borrowing or lending are affected. When they see the discount rate rise, they interpret this as a signal that the Federal Reserve is concerned about the excesses of the boom, and, consequently, they become more cautious in their investment. In addition, with the Federal Reserve fighting inflation there is less reason to expect price rises, and hence there is less of an incentive to undertake anticipatory buying. Conversely, during a recession, a reduction in the discount rate causes both the supply and demand for funds to increase and makes the public less fearful of the recession because it feels that the Federal Reserve is counteracting it. In the Federal Reserve's view the announcement effect of discount rate changes is, therefore, an important tool of countercyclical policy in that it changes expectations in a given direction to help to counteract inflation or recession.

A number of economists have challenged the Federal Reserve's view that the effect of announcing a discount rate is likely to be favorable and have argued that the Federal Reserve could make its message clearer by issuing a forthright statement rather than by requiring the public to interpret the meaning of a change in the discount rate. The message the financial community reads in the change may be vague and even misleading. For example, if the Federal Reserve raises the discount rate merely to keep it in line with the Treasury bill rate, the market may interpret this increase not as a technical adjustment, which it really is, but as an announcement by the Federal Reserve that it wants interest rates in general to rise. (As a rule, the Federal Reserve does not spell out its reasons for changing the discount rate. And even if a Federal Reserve official does give reasons, they may not be accepted by the market but may be treated merely as a smokescreen. Many observers of the money market are "inside-dopesters.") As one critic, Warren Smith, has put it, "the truth is that changes in the discount rate constitute the crudest kind of sign language. Why this stone age form of communication should be regarded as superior to ordinary English is really quite difficult to understand. . . . While a long tradition has perhaps made discount rate increases a reasonably effective means of international communication in some situations of this kind, there are surely other equally satisfactory means available, e.g., English, French, Latin or Zulu." [12]

Moreover, even if the public interprets the change in the discount rate correctly, the announcement may create an opposite effect to that intended by the Federal Reserve and may be destabilizing.[13] The Federal Reserve assumes that when the discount rate rises, lenders expect interest rates to rise further while borrowers expect them to fall. There is little reason to anticipate such a convenient pattern of expectations. A rise in interest rates may cause lenders to expect further rate increases in the future as the Federal Reserve believes—or it may lead them to expect a subsequent fall. A priori, one cannot say which reaction is the more likely. In any case, it is highly improbable that borrowers and lenders would have different expectations, as the Federal Reserve assumes.

Some economists, therefore, have suggested that the discount rate be handled in a way to avoid an announcement effect. This could be done by a technique, tried by Canada at one time as well as by some other countries, of linking the discount rate to the Treasury bill rate, setting it, say, ¼ percent above the bill rate. Changes in the discount rate could then not be misinterpreted—they would clearly *not* signal changes in monetary policy. Member banks could still borrow to replenish reserves, but they would have no incentive to borrow to buy bills. Admittedly, insofar as banks use borrowed funds to hold assets other than Treasury bills, for example commercial paper or busi-

---

[12] Warren L. Smith, "The Instruments of General Monetary Control," *National Banking Review,* Vol. 1 (September, 1963), pp. 60 and 64.

[13] *Ibid.,* pp. 61–64.

ness loans that yield a higher rate of return, these banks may still have an incentive to borrow.

The Reserve Requirement

Nowadays, to economists the primary function of reserve requirements is to limit multiple deposit creation and, through variations of the reserve requirement, to provide the Federal Reserve with a tool of monetary management. Reserve requirements have a long history in American banking. Their original purpose was to protect the depositor, and only gradually did their primary purpose become the limitation of the quantity of money.

For member banks, reserve requirements are set by the Board of Governors within limits established by Congress while the states control the reserve requirements of nonmember banks. State requirements vary widely, ranging from no legal reserve requirement at all in Illinois to 30 percent of demand deposit in Vermont.[14] State requirements tend to be less onerous for banks than Federal Reserve requirements since they allow banks to count as part of their reserve requirement (up to a certain proportion) deposits in other commercial banks, and sometimes United States Government securities, and occasionally even state and local securities. Member banks, on the other hand, can count as reserves only vault cash and deposits with the Federal Reserve. Since they hold government securities and often deposits with other commercial banks in addition to their legal reserve requirement, an equal reserve *ratio* for member and nonmember

[14] However, no part of this 30 percent need be kept in vault cash. See H. P. Gray, "Bank Regulation, Bank Profitability, and Federal Reserve Membership," *National Banking Review*, Vol. 1 (December, 1963), pp. 210–211. These figures relate to 1962.

banks actually imposes a greater burden on member banks. However, quantitatively this differential burden does not seem to be as great as is sometimes supposed.[15]

The Federal Reserve imposes different reserve requirements on member banks depending upon their location (see page 36 below). Banks located in so-called "reserve cities," some fifty major centers, face higher reserve requirements than do banks located elsewhere, the so-called "country banks." Actually, the situation is somewhat more complicated; the Federal Reserve can and does classify many small banks located in reserve cities as country banks. The main criterion for this decision is whether the bank holds substantial deposits of other banks (interbank deposits). Apart from this discrimination among deposits on a (partly) geographic basis, the present system also discriminates greatly between demand deposits and time deposits.

Reserve Requirement Changes

Apart from acting as the fulcrum for open-market operations, the reserve requirement provides an independent tool of monetary policy because the Federal Reserve can change the required reserve ratio. This power was given to the Federal Reserve on a temporary basis by the Banking Act of 1933 and made permanent by the Banking Act of 1935. Under present legislation the Federal Reserve can change reserve requirements of member banks within the following limits:

[15] See Clark Warburton, "Nonmember Banks and the Effectiveness of Monetary Policy," in Commission on Money and Credit, *Monetary Management* (Englewood Cliffs, N.J.: Prentice-Hall, 1963), pp. 346–350.

TABLE 2   *Range of Reserve Requirements*

	Limits Set by Congress		Present Reserve Requirements in Force (April, 1967)
	Minimum	Maximum	
	(Percent)[16]		
Demand Deposits			
Reserve City Banks	10%	22%	16 1/2%
Country Banks	7%	14%	12%
Time Deposits			
All Member Banks	3%	10%	3–6% *

* 3 percent on savings deposits as well as on the first $5 million of other time deposits; otherwise 6 percent.

When the Federal Reserve lowers reserve requirements, the potential money stock is increased in two ways. First, some reserves which were previously required reserves are now excess reserves, and this allows banks to increase their deposits. Second, a lowering of the required reserve ratio raises the deposit multiplier so that any increases in the reserve base allow a greater increase in the money stock than they did before. A raising of the required reserve ratio works, of course, in the opposite direction.

Since the limits within which the Federal Reserve can change the reserve requirements are quite broad, this method of changing the *excess* reserves of banks is very powerful—as in the case of open-market operations, there is plenty of ammunition. But the Federal

[16] Percent of adjusted demand deposits. *Adjusted* demand deposits include, apart from demand deposits, certified checks and cashier's checks outstanding plus letters of credit and traveler's checks sold for cash. The following items are subtracted from this total: demand deposits in incorporated domestic commercial banks, cash items in the process of collection, and cash items on hand to be sent for collection within one day.

Reserve has used its powers to change the reserve requirement only infrequently. In the ten years of 1957 through 1966 the reserve requirement on demand deposits of reserve city banks and country banks was changed only three times for each type of bank, though one should add to this the inclusion of vault cash in reserves as well as the abolition of the central reserve city classification. Thus, the Federal Reserve is using reserve-requirement changes as a method of bringing about broad secular (that is long-run) changes in excess reserves rather than as a sensitive countercyclical device. For example, if a large-scale disarmament program were undertaken, a lowering of reserve requirements would be an obvious way of counteracting the decline in aggregate demand.

In the Federal Reserve's opinion, the power to change reserve requirements does not provide a flexible tool for three reasons. First, reserve-requirement changes cannot be used to bring about small changes in the reserve base since each change in the reserve ratio by ½ percent involves a substantial dollar volume of reserves. Second, every time reserve requirements are raised, banks without sufficient excess reserves are forced to adjust their reserve positions either by liquidating other assets or by borrowing. Naturally, bankers dislike this pressure. Admittedly, this problem occurs only if reserve requirements are raised. If requirements are lowered, banks don't *have* to adjust their portfolios. (To be sure, their optimum portfolio balance changes if reserve requirements are cut, but this occurs also if the Federal Reserve increases reserves via open-market operations.) Third, not only is the process of raising their reserves troublesome for banks, it also requires some time, and hence the Federal Reserve feels that it must give banks some notice before the new, higher reserve requirements become effective. According to the Federal Reserve, raising reserve requirements is therefore a slower acting tool than open-market operations.

It is by no means certain that this reasoning is correct. First, although each change in the reserve ratio by half a percentage point involves a large amount of reserves, why can't the reserve ratio be changed by, say, $\frac{1}{10}$ of 1 percent? [17] Time after time, Federal Reserve statements about the inflexibility of reserve-requirement changes ignore this possibility. Second, if the reserve requirement were raised only by very small steps, then bankers would not find it so hard to meet the new requirement. After all, banks already have to adjust their reserve positions frequently as they experience deposit drains. Finally, if banks are given notice that the reserve requirement will be increased shortly, they will start to adjust their portfolios at once so that at least some of the effect occurs right away. Moreover, if, as will be suggested below, the effect of monetary policy on income occurs only with a fairly substantial lag, the tendency for one tool to take a week or two longer than another is not very significant. Reserve-requirement changes may not be as inflexible a tool as the Federal Reserve believes.

Interaction of Major Tools

Having discussed each of the major tools in isolation, the time has come to see how they interact. There are two aspects of this interaction. On the one hand, each of the tools has its own set of advantages and disadvantages, and they can hence be used to

[17] See Joseph Aschheim, *Techniques of Monetary Control* (Baltimore: Johns Hopkins Press, 1961), p. 20, and Charles Whittlesey, "Reserve Requirements and the Integration of Credit Policies," *Quarterly Journal of Economics,* Vol. 57 (August, 1944), pp. 558–564.

complement each other. On the other hand, since in a broad sense all the tools do the same job, a decision has to be made in each case which one to use, and in this way they are competitive. In its public statements the Federal Reserve has emphasized the complementarity of these tools and has deemphasized their competitive nature.

In the Federal Reserve's view the tools should be used jointly. For example, as a business expansion proceeds, the Federal Reserve may decide to change its policy of "active ease" to a more cautious one.[18] This change will typically occur in small steps. At first, all that may happen is that in making its forecasts of the impact of market forces on bank reserves, the Federal Reserve begins to resolve cases of doubt in the direction of restriction rather than of ease. Thus, the errors that inevitably occur tend to tighten money slightly rather than to ease it. As the expansion continues and the Federal Reserve begins to fear inflation, it purposefully reduces the reserve base by open-market operations. With money tighter and the interest rate rising, the Treasury bill rate exceeds the discount rate. The discount rate is now increased. This is partly a defensive measure to curb bank borrowing and, through the cost element as well as the announcement effect, it serves, in part, to stimulate further increases in market interest rates.[19] If this action proves

---

[18] The Federal Reserve frequently uses terms like "active ease" and may announce, for example, that it is abandoning its policy of "active ease" in favor of a policy of "ease." While the direction of the movement is clear, this type of terminology has no precise and quantitative meaning—at least to people outside the Federal Reserve.

[19] Here is a description of the process given in the 1957 *Annual Report* of the Board of Governors:

In summary, open market policy and discount policy are complementary instruments of day-to-day monetary policy. In a period of monetary restriction, open market policy

insufficient, the Federal Reserve may follow it up with greater open-market sales, or it may, though this recourse is less likely, raise reserve requirements. If it does raise reserve requirements, it may well offset temporarily much of the resulting stringency in the money market by undertaking expansionary open-market operations. These expansionary open-market operations are then reversed over time. In this way excess reserves are reduced in a smooth manner rather than abruptly as they would have been had the Federal Reserve not used open-market purchases to cushion the sharp change in excess reserves resulting from the increase in the reserve ratio.

Once the Federal Reserve feels that the business outlook is changing and that the danger is now more likely to be a recession than an inflation, the Federal Reserve may undertake expansionary open-market operations, which gather force as the recession becomes more and more obvious. (To be sure, if the Federal Reserve is too concerned about inflation, or if it uses the wrong money market indicators, this action may take place only after the recession has gone quite far —a point made by many critics of the Federal Reserve.) As market rates of interest fall, the discount

---

limits the availability of bank reserves at the System's initiative. In effect this action places initiative in obtaining additional reserves with the member banks, many of which are reluctant to operate for extended periods on the basis of borrowed reserves. As restrictive monetary policy continues or becomes more intense, there are increases in the frequency, average duration, and volume of discounts, as well as in the number of member banks engaged in such borrowing. At such times, the cost of borrowing reserves —that is, the discount rate—may also be raised. Commercial bank lending and investing policies thus come under increasing restraint.

Quoted in David Eastburn, *The Federal Reserve on Record* (Philadelphia: Federal Reserve Board of Philadelphia, n.d.), p. 100.

rate is again out of line with market rates, and the gap between it and the market rates discourages borrowing. This situation is deflationary, and so the Federal Reserve is likely to lower the discount rate. Moreover, since, in any case, the money supply must be increased due to the secular expansion of the economy, the Federal Reserve may lower the reserve-requirement ratio, cushioning the move by open-market sales at the same time.

But this picture of smooth orchestration of monetary instruments is only half the story; it leaves out the competitive element. At each step the Federal Reserve has to make a choice of which of its tools to use. This choice frequently involves considerations other than those of monetary management in the narrow sense. Let us, therefore, look at the relative advantages and disadvantages of each of the major tools. To do this we treat cyclical and secular policy actions separately. In addition to following a countercyclical, that is short-run, policy the Federal Reserve also has the task of providing for a secular growth of the money stock. With output rising over time, price stability requires a secular increase in the money stock unless velocity (the average number of times each dollar of money becomes income per year) is rising sufficiently. In practice, cyclical and secular elements tend to fuse— for example, the Federal Reserve may take care of the secular growth of the money stock, in part, by lowering reserve requirements during a recession and then by not raising them during the expansion. But although cyclical and secular elements may be combined into one policy, one can analyze them separately.

Relative Advantages and Disadvantages of Major Tools for Countercyclical Policy

To start with the countercyclical problem, let us compare the relative advantages and disadvantages of discount rate changes, open-market operations, and reserve-requirement changes. Comparing the first two of these, open-market operations have three clear-cut advantages over discount rate changes: First, open-market operations are much stronger and can bring about much bigger changes in the reserve base than can discount rate changes; second, they are more flexible; and third, they are much more precise. Unlike discount rate changes, the Federal Reserve can undertake open-market operations to change the reserve base by the exact amount it wants. Discount rate changes, on the other hand, merely vary the incentives which banks have to borrow—the Federal Reserve has no way of knowing exactly by how much they will change their borrowing. In addition, open-market operations have less of an announcement effect than do discount rate changes. Some observers have stressed this point strongly, believing that the announcement effect is *much* greater for discount rate changes than it is for open-market operations. But note that the important financial decisions are made by sophisticated people who are quite aware of what the Federal Reserve is doing in the open market. Admittedly, discount rate changes tend to make the observed changes in the money market "official" so that in this way their announcement does have a greater effect. In any case, as pointed out above, whether this effect is an advantage or not is debatable. But, on the other hand, discount rate changes probably have a wider immediate geographical impact than open-market operations.

In comparing discount rate changes with reserve-requirement changes, one finds that the latter have more strength. At least in the range within which the Federal Reserve has varied the discount rate, its effects on bank reserves are distinctly smaller than those that can be achieved with reserve-requirement changes. It is not easy to decide which one of these two tools is the more precise. Reserve-requirement changes are more precise in the sense that the Federal Reserve knows exactly by how much it is changing required reserves. On the other hand, given the Federal Reserve's penchant for changing reserve requirements only by relatively large steps, discount rates can be used for smaller adjustments because they are more precise. (Note, however, that this precision is largely a reflection of the fact that discount rate changes are not as powerful a tool as reserve-requirement changes.) Rightly or wrongly, the Federal Reserve seems to feel that discount rate changes are a more flexible weapon than reserve-requirement changes—at least the Federal Reserve has used them more flexibly. To summarize, discount rate changes are weaker than the other two major tools, and, while less flexible than open-market operations, they are, at least in the Federal Reserve's opinion, more flexible than reserve-requirement changes. Let us then turn to a comparison between open-market operations and reserve-requirement changes.

Reserve-requirement changes have two advantages over open-market operations as a countercyclical tool. First, reserve-requirement changes have a full geographic impact without a significant lag. As mentioned above, open-market operations may take a longer time to spread the effects to banks throughout the country. A second advantage is that banks are more willing to expand their loans and deposits if they gain excess reserves through a cut in the reserve requirement rather than through open-market operations. Unless the bank itself sells securities, Federal Reserve open-market purchases show up for the individual bank as an increase in the deposits of customers who have sold securities. The bank has no way of knowing for how long it will have these deposits; it has experienced an abnormal increase in deposits and may now expect to face an abnormal drain. When reserve requirements are lowered, however, the bank acquires excess reserves and has no reason to expect an abnormal deposit drain; hence it is more willing to use these reserves. To be sure, one could well argue that this difference is not very important—if banks are less willing to expand on the basis of a dollar of reserves generated by open-market operations than by reserve requirement changes, the Federal Reserve could simply offset this tendency by buying more securities, so that this advantage seems rather minor.

Against the two advantages of reserve-requirement changes over open-market operations mentioned above one has to balance several disadvantages. First, reserve-requirement changes cannot be undertaken anywhere near as frequently as open-market operations—continuous changes would make life too hard for banks and drive many out of the Federal Reserve System. Second, the Federal Reserve has argued that reserve requirements cannot be changed by small steps. But, as pointed out above, this reservation is dubious.

Third, and finally, according to the Federal Reserve, increases in reserve requirements, unlike open-market sales, create problems for banks. If reserve requirements are raised, all banks are affected regardless of whether they have excess reserves, and those banks without excess reserves must reduce loans, sell securities, or borrow. By contrast, if the Federal Reserve sells securities, banks without excess reserves need not buy any securities. But this is only partially correct. Open-market sales reduce the reserves even of those banks that do not themselves participate in the open-market transactions. If their deposit customers buy securities, their reserves are reduced. But the Federal Reserve *may* have something else in mind. If reserve requirements are raised, banks facing a shortage of reserves know that the Federal Reserve is to blame for their trouble, but banks that lose reserves because their customers buy securities do not know that the Federal Reserve's open-market operations are responsible.[20] Since the Federal Reserve likes to live at peace with its member banks, open-market operations make life easier for the Federal Reserve than do reserve-requirement increases.

To summarize this discussion, Table 3 shows the salient advantages of each of these tools.

Relative Advantages and Disadvantages of Various Tools for Secular Changes

In addition to changing bank reserves over the cycle, the Federal Reserve also has an obligation to allow for a secular (that is, long-run) increase in the money stock as output and velocity change over time. This secular problem is easier to solve in one respect: Discount rate changes can be ignored. Given the reluctance of banks to borrow and the reluctance of the Federal Reserve to permit a bank to stay permanently in debt, even a continually falling discount rate would

[20] For a statement by Chairman William Martin which lends itself to this interpretation, see Eastburn, *op. cit.,* p. 134.

TABLE 3 Relative Advantages of Various Monetary Tools for Countercyclical Actions

	Discount Rate Changes	Open-Market Operations	Discount Rate Changes	Reserve Requirement Changes	Reserve Requirement Changes	Open-Market Operations
Strength		X		X	—[1]	—[1]
Flexibility		X	P?[2]	P?[2]		X
Precision		X	P?[3]	P?[3]		X
Faster Geographic Spread	X		—	—	X	
Willingness of Banks to Change Assets	—	—	—	—	X	

Good Relations with Commercial Banks	—	—	X⁴	X⁴
Relative Strength of Announcement⁵ Effect	X	—	—	X

X denotes superiority

— denotes approximate equality

[1] Both have more than adequate strength.

[2] The relative flexibility of these two tools is uncertain. The Federal Reserve appears to believe that discount rate changes are the more flexible tool and, hence, uses this tool more flexibly.

[3] The relative precision of these two tools is uncertain. Given present Federal Reserve practices, discount rate changes are probably more precise. With a different Federal Reserve policy, reserve requirement changes may be more precise.

[4] This factor applies to increases, not to decreases, in reserve requirements.

[5] Whether a strong announcement effect is desirable is uncertain.

not suffice to increase the money stock enough in the long run.

In deciding between open-market operations and reserve-requirement changes, the factors discussed above in connection with countercyclical actions are not relevant for secular increases in the money stock;[21] instead, what is significant is the distribution of gains between the Treasury and commercial banks. If the money supply is increased secularly by lowering reserve requirements, banks are enabled to purchase additional earning assets without relinquishing any securities they already hold. On the other hand, if the Federal Reserve increases reserves by buying securities from banks, the banks obtain additional reserves only by giving up some of their securities. Interest on these securities is now paid by the Treasury, not to the commercial banks but to the Federal Reserve, which in turn hands it back to the Treasury.

The same thing holds if the Federal Reserve buys securities from nonbanks. The seller deposits the sales proceeds in his bank, and bank reserves are increased. Both assets and liabilities of the bank rise. The bank is worse off than it would have been had reserve requirements been reduced instead, for a reduction in reserve requirements would have raised the bank's earning assets without raising its deposit liabilities.

Not surprisingly, this problem became a political issue, and the Federal Reserve was criticized in the

---

[21] The fact that the impact of open-market operations is geographically concentrated is not relevant because in the long run the effects spread throughout the country. Similarly, the fact that changes in reserve requirements are more obvious to the banks is not important—eventually they will find out that the increase in their reserves is permanent. Lowering the reserve requirement continuously does not upset banks and, in any case, secular changes do not necessitate proceeding by continuous small steps; discontinuous large steps offset by temporary open-market operations can do the job.

late 1950's for taking care of the secular increase in the money stock at that time primarily by lowering reserve requirements rather than by open-market purchases. The Federal Reserve replied to its critics that it is *not* the function of a central bank to earn income for the Treasury. It is a basic principle of central banking that the central bank should conduct its operations with complete disregard of profit and loss. But the critics answered that while it is certainly true that a central bank should put the stabilization goal *ahead* of any desire to earn income, if there are two ways of changing bank reserves which do the job *equally* efficiently, then the central bank may legitimately take its earnings into account in choosing between them.

This argument, however, is open to an objection. If the Federal Reserve pays attention to its earnings when they make no difference to its stabilization function, there is a danger that, over time, it will gradually drift into a position of taking its earnings into account even in those cases when it shouldn't.

In addition, while it is possible to separate analytically secular and cyclical increases in the reserve base, in day-to-day operations they present a single unit of action. Thus, if the Federal Reserve wants to increase the reserve base during a cyclical downturn, it *may* want to do so by lowering reserve requirements perhaps because reserve-requirement changes have a broader geographic impact. Then during the expansion, when the Federal Reserve wants to restrict the growth of the reserve base, it *may* want to use open-market operations, perhaps because they are more rapidly implemented than reserve-requirement changes. If the Federal Reserve cuts reserve requirements during the recession and does not raise them in the expansion, there is a secular downward drift in the reserve ratio, and purely as a by-product of choosing the best countercyclical action the Federal Reserve finds itself providing for the secular growth of the money stock by lowering reserve requirements. In other words, it is certainly *possible* that the Federal Reserve faces an asymmetry; cutting reserve requirements may be superior to open-market operations as an expansionary policy during a recession, but open-market operations may be preferable to raising reserve requirements as a countercyclical policy during the upswing. This course of action is certainly a *possibility;* whether it is more than a possibility is, of course, highly debatable. But it does suggest that one *may* be incorrect to argue that since changes in reserve requirements and open-market purchases are equally effective tools of secular expansion, the only relevant consideration is the impact on government finance.

Are All These Tools Necessary?

Having discussed which of the three major tools to use both for cyclical and for secular purposes, we turn to one remaining problem. This is the basic issue whether all three tools are really necessary. Thus, Smith has suggested that after reserve requirements are established at the optimal level, a desirable course may be to eliminate for normal times the power to change reserve requirements. Milton Friedman would go even further and would abolish not only the power to change reserve requirements but also the power to discount, leaving the Federal Reserve only one tool: open-market operations. In his view, open-market operations are perfectly adequate to change the reserve base. Giving the central bank more than a single tool merely confuses the issue.[22]

[22] Milton Friedman, *A Program for Monetary Stability* (New York: Fordham University Press, 1960), pp. 30–51.

Although in principle it is certainly correct that open-market operations alone could be used to change the reserve base, the Federal Reserve feels that it is able to use all three tools in combination in an effective manner. To a considerable extent, though not completely, this question is involved in a larger issue. As is discussed below, Friedman would have the central bank abandon countercyclical policy and would have it do only one thing: raise the money stock at a steady rate. For such a policy, little would be gained by having two other tools in addition to open-market operations. And even considering the present goals of monetary policy it is by no means clear that three tools do the job better than one tool would.[23]

Before leaving the comparison of major tools, we should note that the above analysis deals only with the United States and does not necessarily apply to other countries. For example, in many countries the discount rate is more important than in the United States. In Japan it is the primary tool of monetary policy, and in Britain, too, the bank rate is more important than is the discount rate in the United States; not only business loans, but even interest rates on out-

[23] Viner has argued that in a system such as America's, which has a large number of small banks, the discount privilege is necessary since small banks may face substantial deposit drains and do not have easy access to the money market ("The Necessity and Desirable Range of Discretion to be Allowed to a Monetary Authority," in Leland Yeager [ed.], *In Search of A Monetary Constitution* [Cambridge: Harvard University Press, 1962], p. 260). But the difference between Friedman and Viner on this issue is not as great as it may seem. Under present regulations, banks not meeting their reserve requirements are subject to a fine. This fine could act like the discount mechanism if banks could somehow be induced to look upon the imposition of such a fine as a normal thing and not as a reflection on their virtue. A discount rate kept significantly higher than the bill rate would have a similar effect.

standing mortgages are linked to it. The Swiss central bank relies primarily on discount rate changes; until a few years ago it did not even have the legal power to undertake open-market operations. Moreover, in many developed as well as underdeveloped countries open-market operations are not feasible because the government security market is too thin and inadequate. Open-market operations are a full-fledged tool of monetary policy in only a few countries, notably the United States, Britain, and Canada.[24]

Selective Controls

The major monetary tools discussed above are methods of changing bank reserves and, hence, aggregate demand throughout the economy. Another set of tools focuses on specific areas of the economy. These "selective" controls have their initial impact on specific markets rather than on the whole economy. They do not possess one frequently claimed advantage of monetary policy, neutrality,[25] but instead affect particular markets that are claimed to be relatively insulated from the effects of over-all monetary policy. These controls are designed to focus on trouble spots where demand may be excessive; their characteristics are those of a rifle, not of a shotgun.

At present there are only two selective controls, Regulations T and U.[26] They limit stock market credit

[24] Peter Fousek, *Foreign Central Banking: The Instruments of Monetary Policy* (New York: Federal Reserve Bank of New York, 1957), p. 31. See also Graeme Dorrance, "The Instruments of Monetary Policy in Countries without Highly Developed Capital Markets," *Staff Papers*, Vol. 12 (July, 1965), pp. 272–278.

[25] The meaning of neutrality, as well as its advantages and disadvantages, are discussed in Chapter 4.

[26] Strictly speaking, Regulation A covering the types of paper the Federal Reserve is willing to discount is also a "selective

extended by security brokers and banks, respectively. The method used is to set a minimum margin requirement, that is, to set a minimum down payment for stocks registered on national security exchanges. At present (1967) the margin requirement is 70 percent. This means that the purchaser must put up at least 70 percent of the value of the stock himself and may borrow only 30 percent from his bank or broker. The Federal Reserve has the power to vary the margin requirement and can raise it up to 100 percent to control a speculative stock market boom.

The reason the Federal Reserve was given this power by the Securities and Exchange Act in 1934 can be seen by looking back at the situation in 1927–1929. In these years the Wholesale Price Index was stable, but there was a speculative boom in the stock market. The Federal Reserve was in a quandary. It had no power to affect the stock market directly. By raising the discount rate or by open-market operations it could make credit generally less available and, hence, would to some extent limit the purchase of stocks on credit. But with stock prices rising rapidly, even a substantial boost in interest rates would be unlikely to have much effect on stock market borrowing. And such a substantial rise in interest rates would have been deflationary for the rest of the economy. At first, the Federal Reserve relied on moral suasion to limit stock market loans of banks, and then later it raised the discount rate moderately. This rise in the discount rate was too little and too late to curb the stock mar-

---

control" but since Regulation A is fairly general, it is usually not included in the list of "selective controls." The designations "Regulation T" and "Regulation U" come from the fact that when the Federal Reserve commenced operations it issued a series of regulations starting with "Regulation A" (discounting) and had reached the letters T and U by the time it issued the stock market margin regulations.

ket boom. If the Federal Reserve had had Regulations
T and U at that time it could have limited stock market credit without a deflationary effect on the rest of
the economy.

As people so often do, the government locked the
barn door after the horse was stolen. Since 1934 there
has been no disastrous speculative boom in the stock
market and, although the margin requirement was on
occasion raised to 100 percent, it was probably not a
very important factor. An empirical study of Regulations T and U suggests that they have not succeeded
in reducing fluctuation and risk in the stock market
or in limiting an "excessive" use of credit for security
purchases.[27] Moreover, in recent years the growth of
unregulated security lenders has weakened the impact
of Regulations T and U.

Potentially much more important are selective controls over consumer credit. During World War II, as
well as during the Korean War and briefly in 1948–
1949, the Federal Reserve set minimum down payments and maximum maturities for loans for consumer
durable purchases (Regulation W). At present, the
Federal Reserve does not have the legal power to control consumer credit although in England and in some
other countries consumer credit control is used as a
countercyclical weapon.

From time to time a number of economists have proposed reinstituting consumer credit controls. This idea
gathered considerable support in 1955 when consumer
credit rose rapidly in spite of a restrictive monetary
policy. Since then, support for reinstituting Regulation
W has waned. However, there has been some Congressional interest. The latest instance is a favorable report

[27] See Thomas Moore, "Stock Market Margin Requirements,"
Journal of Political Economy, Vol. 74 (April, 1966), pp. 158–
167.

by the House Banking and Currency Committee on a bill that included standby authority for the President to regulate consumer credit.

The advocates of Regulation W point to several advantages of regulating consumer credit directly. First, consumer credit is a destabilizing factor since credit purchases conform positively to the business cycle. Given the size of credit sales in our economy, they are a significant destabilizer. Second, the argument runs, consumer credit extension is almost immune to monetary policy. Hence, conventional monetary policy puts a greatly disproportionate part of the burden of curbing aggregate demand on investment and too little on consumption. Another argument for using consumer credit controls is that they take less time to become effective than general controls since they affect consumption rather than investment. (The importance of quick response is discussed in Chapter 4 below.)

One other point that seems to dispose some people favorably to Regulation W is a belief that some consumers act irrationally in using consumer credit.

There is, however, a good deal to be said for the other side of this dispute. First, it is a debatable issue whether the conventional tools of monetary policy are really powerless to affect consumer credit significantly. At the same time it can be argued that consumer credit controls have much less effect than appears at first on *total* demand—if banks make fewer consumer loans, they are in a better position to make business loans. Moreover, one can argue that monetary policy should not disturb resource allocation, that it should concern itself only with aggregate demand and not with demand in any particular sector of the economy. In addition, consumer credit controls raise serious equity problems since they discriminate against households unable to meet the down payment requirement. Another difficulty with consumer credit controls is that they raise very substantial enforcement problems; this type of regulation can be evaded fairly easily. Finally, one may object to consumer credit controls on political grounds since they are a serious interference with economic freedom.

Moral Suasion and Direct Action

Another minor tool in the Federal Reserve's armory is moral suasion, sometimes called "open mouth policy" or "jaw control." This simply means that the Federal Reserve uses its powers of persuasion to get banks or the financial community in general to behave differently. Since the interests of the Federal Reserve frequently coincide with the long-run self-interest of financial institutions, this form of control may *in certain cases* be more effective than it appears to be at first. For example, during an inflationary expansion, the Federal Reserve may urge lenders to be more cautious in their loan policies, and lenders may treat this as sound business advice from someone who can forecast business conditions better than they can. To be sure, sometimes banks and other institutions may feel that the stress is more on the "suasion" than on the "moral." For example, in 1965 when the President and the Federal Reserve laid down guidelines to limit foreign lending, some banks, at least according to some reports, were afraid that if they ignored the guidelines, they might find it more difficult to borrow from the Federal Reserve. Admittedly, these fears may have been groundless, but for an outsider it is hard to say.

Direct action means that the Federal Reserve can bring pressure to bear on particular member banks whose actions it considers undesirable. Clearly, direct action is a method for keeping a few black sheep in line rather than for controlling the great thundering herd of banks.

Publicity and Informal Advice

The Federal Reserve has many ways of making its opinions known to the general public. The Chairman of the Board of Governors is frequently invited to testify before Congressional committees, and press releases by the Federal Reserve are given attention by journalists. In addition, the Board of Governors publishes each month the *Federal Reserve Bulletin,* and all twelve Federal Reserve Banks publish a monthly review. Given the high regard in which the business community and its journalists hold the Federal Reserve, the central bank has no difficulty in getting its views and opinions across to the public.

These means of communication give the Federal Reserve some influence over business expectations— exactly how much influence is hard to say. Some economists, though by no means all, attach a great deal of importance to expectations; they believe that, at least to a considerable extent, expectations tend to justify themselves. For example, if the Federal Reserve were to announce that it expects long-term interest rates to rise, lenders would refrain from buying long-term bonds, waiting for the rate to rise, while borrowers would try to float securities right away before the rate rose. Given such an increase in the demand for long-term funds and a decline in the supply, the interest rate would rise right away.

Finally, the Federal Reserve need not confine its publicity to the general public. The Chairman of the Board of Governors acts as one of the chief economic and financial advisors of the President. At present

(1967) there is an informal economic "general staff" in Washington that meets with the President. It consists of the Secretary of the Treasury, the Chairman of the Council of Economic Advisers, the Director of the Budget Bureau—and the Chairman of the Board of Governors. A strong chairman who has good relations with the President can exercise a great deal of influence in this way.

These, then, are the domestic tools of the Federal Reserve: Open-market operations, discount rate changes, and reserve requirement changes carry the bulk of the burden; and they are reinforced by selective controls, moral suasion, direct action, publicity, and informal advice.

International Tools

The Federal Reserve tries to meet its international responsibilities in several ways. One is to change interest rates and income by using the domestic tools just discussed. Another way is to further international liquidity by collaborating with foreign central banks in so-called "swap operations." In these operations a central bank under temporary pressure can swap its own currency against foreign currency, and, hence. it can obtain funds to ride out a speculative attack or other temporary factors. In addition, the Federal Reserve collaborates with other leading nations' central banks in trying to stabilize the gold market and deals in the forward exchange market to stabilize that market. Central banks of various nations also collaborate on a more general issue: interest rates. In setting their interest rates, central banks look not only at their own economy, but, at times, take at least some account of the effect of their actions on other countries.

In addition, the Federal Reserve also has the task of

administering the guidelines on foreign loans by banks. Since it is the agency dealing directly with the banks likely to make substantial foreign loans (since such banks tend to be member banks) it is the government agency best equipped to do this.[28]

Finally, the Federal Reserve, which has a large staff of economists doing research on international financial problems and on foreign economies, advises the President on international financial decisions.

APPENDIX TO CHAPTER 2

Debt Management

In addition to the tools of monetary policy that the Federal Reserve possesses, the Treasury Department has one major monetary stabilization tool that has received considerable attention in the postwar period. This is debt management.[1] Our national debt is large and a significant part of it, close to half of the marketable debt, consists of short-term securities due within a year. Treasury sales and redemptions of debt, therefore, amount to a substantial sum each year. As the Treasury borrows it has to decide whether to issue long-term or short-term securities. This is the essence of debt management. Note that debt management re-

[28] These exchange controls are, in a way, selective controls. However, I have not grouped them with other selective controls since their purpose is so very different.

[1] For an excellent discussion of debt management see Warren Smith, "Debt Management in the United States," *Employment, Growth and Price Levels,* U.S. Congress, Joint Economic Committee, Study Paper #19 (Washington, D.C.: 86th Congress, Second Session, 1960).

fers to changes in the *composition* of the debt, not to the total volume of debt outstanding. The volume of debt outstanding changes in accordance with deficit or surplus in the budget and, hence, is fiscal policy. Debt management, on the other hand, is essentially monetary since its effects on aggregate demand operate through the changing of people's demand for money or changes in interest rates.

Shifting the debt between long-term and short-term securities can affect aggregate demand. There are two ways to approach this. One is to say that if the public holds short-term rather than long-term securities it is more willing to spend because its holdings are more liquid. Short-term government securities can serve as money substitutes. Put into Keynesian language, the public need not hold money to satisfy either precautionary or speculative motives, but can hold short-term securities instead. In some cases short-term securities serve as a money substitute even for transaction balances. Hence, if the Treasury issues short-term securities in place of long-term government securities, the demand for money drops, and the interest rate declines.

Another approach to the effects of changes in the maturity composition of the debt is to look at the term structure of interest rates. If the Treasury redeems long-term bonds and issues short-term securities in their place, this reduction in outstanding long-term securities tends, at least initially, to lower the long-term rate of interest. On the other hand, the greater supply of short-term securities raises the short-term rate of interest, at least initially. Many, though not all, economists believe that the long-term interest rate has more effect on investment decisions than does the short-term rate. Hence, as the Treasury redeems long-term securities and issues short-term securities, the effect of the decline in the long-term rate is not fully offset by the effect of the rise in the short-term rate, and investment increases. Conversely, if the Treasury wants to restrain aggregate demand it should redeem short-term securities and issue long-term securities instead. Here, then, may be a method of influencing aggregate demand, a method that could supplement the tools used by the Federal Reserve. In the early postwar period when debt management was first brought to public attention, this new control mechanism aroused considerable enthusiasm, but for several reasons this enthusiasm has cooled in recent years.

One obvious problem is the behavior of the term structure of interest rates. Whether changes in the composition of the debt can have any *lasting* effect on the term structure of interest rates is a matter of dispute.[2] Empirical evidence can be cited for either view. Similarly, while there is little dispute about the direction of the effect on expenditures of issuing short-term securities in place of long-term securities, there is still considerable dispute as to whether this effect is of significant size.[3] Another problem is that selling long-

[2] Some economists stress the ability of security buyers and sellers to shift between markets. They believe that a change in relative interest rates brought about by debt management is only transitory and is eliminated by arbitrage. Some other economists, however, argue that the long-term and short-term markets are sufficiently insulated from each other to allow debt management to change the relation of long-term and short-term interest rates.

[3] An additional disadvantage of countercyclical debt management is that it is very slow. Not only does it suffer from the usual lags in the effectiveness of monetary policy discussed in Chapter 4, but there is an additional lag. If long-term securities are issued during the expansion, these long-term securities stay in the debt structure during the next contraction and tend to reduce expenditures at that time too. A long time passes until these new long-term securities are redeemed so that a contractionary debt policy, unlike an expansionary debt policy, is *not* easily reversible.

term securities in the expansion when interest rates are high, and selling short-term securities during the recession when interest rates are low, serves to lock high interest rate securities into the debt structure, and thus to raise interest costs to the Treasury. Secretaries of the Treasury tend to take a dim view of this. Still another problem is created by the fact that if the Treasury sells short-term securities in the recession, these short-term security holdings by the public interfere with a subsequent tightening of monetary policy in the expansion. As is discussed further in Chapter 3, holders of these short-term securities can sell them to owners of idle balances and obtain the wherewithal for increasing their expenditures. Moreover, a short-term debt requires frequent Treasury refinancing, and such refinancing interferes with monetary policy. During a refinancing period the Federal Reserve is reluctant to tighten money, but tries to help the Treasury financing by keeping the bond market on an "even keel." A large short-term debt severely restricts the times when the Federal Reserve feels free to move in a restrictive direction. Given these problems with countercyclical debt management a number of economists advocate putting as much as possible of the debt into long-term securities. Debt management then does not help directly in economic stabilization, but at least it minimizes the difficulties which a large debt creates for monetary policy. Still another group of economists favor using as the goal of debt management minimizing the interest cost to the Treasury.

Chapter **3** | # The Strength of Monetary Policy

Contrary to the opinions of many contemporary economists (and to some of my own earlier views) I believe that monetary and credit policies have great potency to stimulate, stabilize or depress a modern economy. This belief is based on my evaluation of the tremendous amount of empirical data given by (1) history, (2) current statistics, and (3) case studies of business behavior. These data are diverse, conflicting, and often inconclusive, and therefore have to be interpreted with the help of all the tools of economic analysis inherited from the past and developed by the present generation of scholars. **Paul A. Samuelson**[1]

Bank Reserves and the Money Stock

The previous chapter dealt with the methods the Federal Reserve uses to change bank reserves. But, in and of themselves, changes in bank reserves are unimportant. They are important only because they lead to subsequent changes in the money stock and in

[1] Paul A. Samuelson, "Reflections on Central Banking," *National Banking Review*, Vol. 1 (September, 1963), p. 15.

income. The magnitude of the effect of changes in bank reserves on income is still quite controversial and forms the subject of this chapter.

To start, let us look at the effect of changes in reserves on the stock of money. There are several approaches to this topic. One approach, a quite traditional one, is the simple process of multiple deposit creation described in money and banking textbooks. Banks obtain reserves and expand the money supply to a multiple of these reserves. There is a simple and direct relation between reserves and the money stock. Another approach, which became popular in the 1930's, was to argue that banks usually have some excess reserves so that the volume of reserves is usually not an operative restraint on the volume of deposits; instead the deposit volume depends on the demand for bank credit. According to this view, changes in the reserve base will frequently have little effect on stock of money.

In recent years, a more sophisticated approach has been developed, which takes something from each of the older approaches. On the one hand, it uses a money multiplier (the link between the reserve base and the money stock) to go from the reserve base to the stock of money. On the other, this money multiplier is not taken as a constant but depends in part on the demand for bank credit. The demand for bank credit is one of the variables affecting the rate of interest, and the rate of interest, in turn, affects the size of the money multiplier. In a realistic model the money multiplier depends not only on the required reserve ratio, but also on the bank's desire for excess reserves and interbank deposits and on the public's demand for time deposits—factors influenced by the interest rate. Another important determinant of the money multiplier is the public's demand for currency, which depends mainly on income.

To determine how strong the Federal Reserve monetary policy is two questions must be answered: First, is there a stable money multiplier in the sense that the Federal Reserve can rely on the money stock changing significantly and predictably as it changes bank reserves? Second, how large is this money multiplier? Much, though not all, recent empirical research suggests that there is a predictable money multiplier but that its value is fairly low, about two to three and a half, and not between six or seven as it would be if the legal reserve requirement were the only leakage. But the fact that the money multiplier is low does not seriously hinder the Federal Reserve. All it has to do is to change the reserve base by a larger amount than would be necessary if the money multiplier were larger.

Money, Interest Rates, and Investment

If the money supply does change with changes in reserves one could argue in quantity theory fashion that the Federal Reserve can have a very powerful effect on income. According to the quantity theory monetary policy is not hindered by inadequate strength.

Another possibility is to analyze the problem of the strength of monetary policy along more Keynesian lines. In the Keynesian system an increase in the stock of money lowers the rate of interest, and this lowering of the interest rate brings about an increase in investment which in turn leads to an increase in income. Thus in the Keynesian system, as in the quantity theory, an increase in the stock of money raises income, and a decline in the stock of money lowers income. But there is a very important difference in the two theories here. In the quantity theory, changes in the stock of money dominate income, whereas in the Keynesian theory, changes in the money stock have a much smaller effect on income, and, besides, the stock of money is only one of many variables determining income. Thus, the Keynesian looks upon monetary policy as having less strength than the quantity theorist believes it has.

One factor that weakens monetary policy is that since the Federal Reserve undertakes its open-market operations primarily in short-term securities, the direct impact of monetary policy is mainly on the short-term interest rate. (To be sure, this impact is not wholly limited to short-term interest rates. Some of the increase in bank reserves may lead to an increase in the demand for long-term securities.) Changes in the short-term interest rate do have *some* effect on the long-term interest rate, but the effect tends to be, at least in the short run, rather small. The long-term rate of interest fluctuates much less than the short-term rate. In the Keynesian system it is primarily the long-term rate of interest that affects investment, so that some of the effectiveness of the monetary policy in changing income is lost in this transition from the short-term rate to the long-term rate.

Moreover, there is another problem that arises *if prices are inflexible*. An increase in the quantity of money lowers the rate of interest, and at this lower rate of interest the public wants to hold a greater quantity of money per dollar of income—this is the famous Keynesian liquidity preference relation. As a result, only one part of the effect of a rise in the quantity of money goes to increase the level of income; the other part goes to increase the amount of money held per dollar of income, that is, to decrease velocity in quantity theory language. At one extreme, cases A or B in Figure 1, where either liquidity preference is

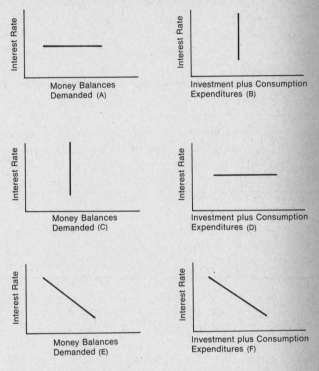

Figure 1. The Interest Rate, Demand for Money, and Expenditures.

NOTE: A or B represent income completely unaffected by changes in the quantity of money; C or D represent income completely determined by the money stock; and E and F represent changes in the money stock having some effect on income, but less than in C or D.

completely interest elastic or expenditures are completely interest inelastic, changing the quantity of money has no effect at all on income. At the other extreme, cases C or D illustrated in Figure 1, liquidity preference is completely interest inelastic or expenditures are perfectly interest elastic. In these cases, the Keynesian and quantity theories give the same answer: income changes in proportion to the stock of money. Between these two extremes are the empirically more pertinent cases, cases E and F, where income does change in response to changes in the money supply but does so less than proportionately.

Evidence developed in recent statistical studies generally rejects the extremes of A, B, C, or D. Such studies suggest that liquidity preference does *not* become infinite even at low rates of interest but, on the other hand, that it is not completely interest inelastic either. Similarly, expenditures show some, but by no means infinite, interest elasticity. The intermediate cases, cases E and F, are the empirically relevant ones.

Various studies of the interest elasticity of the liquidity preference relation have come up with different estimates, but generally these estimates tend to be about unity or less. As for the interest elasticity of expenditures, many, though by no means all, economists feel that consumption has not much interest inelasticity, while about investment there is more controversy. In the 1920's economists generally thought that investment was very responsive to changes in the interest rate, but in the 1930's opinion changed radically. There were several reasons for this change of opinion. One was the argument that for short-term investment the interest rate is only a minor cost element, while for long-range investment changes in the interest rate are rendered unimportant by the great uncertainty involved in long-term investment. Moreover, studies undertaken at that time found that investment was quite unresponsive to interest rates. Finally, most economists interpreted the Great Depression as showing that easy money does not suffice to raise the economy out of a slump.

In recent years there has been a great burgeoning of research in this area, and conclusions reached in the 1930's and 1940's are being challenged. Thus, a re-interpretation of the 1930's argues that money was *not* easy then so that the Great Depression, far from proving the unimportance of money, demonstrated its importance.[2] Similarly, a number of sophisticated statistical studies of industrial plant and equipment investment have been undertaken in recent years, and a number of them, though by no means all, have found that the interest rate does have a significant effect on investment.[3] Moreover, there is widespread agreement that monetary factors are quite important for one major investment sector: residential construction.

So much for the case of price inflexibility. The opposite situation of completely flexible prices where the change in income takes the form of price level changes is quite different. Unless the liquidity preference curve is infinitely elastic, or investment and consumption completely interest inelastic (A or B in Figure 1), a change in the stock of money causes a proportionate change in money income. Suppose that the stock of money is increased. If so, the rate of interest falls initially. As a result the public moves down along the liquidity preference schedule and decides to hold a greater real quantity of money.

[2] The main work here is Milton Friedman and Anna Schwartz, *A Monetary History of the United States, 1867–1960* (Princeton: Princeton University Press, 1963), Chs. 7–9. For a brief summary of the debate, see author's *Monetary Policy in the United States* (New York: Random House, in preparation), Appendix B.

[3] For documentation, see my *Monetary Policy in the United States, op. cit.*, p. 122–123 n.

Hence, as with price inflexibility, expenditures and money income initially rise less than in proportion to the increase in the money stock. But since expenditures do rise to some extent and prices are flexible, the price level rises. This increase in the price level lowers the real value of the money stock and continues to do so as long as the interest rate is below its (full employment-price stability) equilibrium, that is, until the money stock in real terms has declined back to its original level. At this new equilibrium point, the real money stock being unchanged, the rate of interest is back to where it was originally and so is the public's demand for money balances. Thus in this case of price flexibility, as long as the liquidity preference curve is not infinitely elastic or the expenditure curve completely interest inelastic money income rises in proportion to the money stock regardless of the particular values of the elasticities. Conversely, if the nominal money stock is reduced, money income falls proportionately.[4]

But to a large extent monetary policy is concerned with the short run, and most economists, though not all, believe that in the short run there is a considerable price inflexibility.[5]

The Availability Doctrine

In addition to the just discussed effects operating through the interest rate, monetary policy also affects investment through manipulating the sheer availability

[4] Moreover, insofar as price increases tend to make the public expect further price increases, the (money) rate of interest rises above its previous level. See Milton Friedman, "Interest Rates and the Demand for Money," *Journal of Law and Economics,* Vol. 9 (October, 1966), pp. 71–86.

[5] Friedman believes that there is enough price flexibility so that an increase in the money supply soon raises interest rates.

of credit to borrowers. The credit market is a highly imperfect one; a borrower cannot obtain the quantity of credit he wants merely by offering to pay the prevailing price (interest rate). Instead, banks and other lenders ration credit. In a period of tight money they turn down loan applicants and reduce the amounts and maturities of loans they do make. Hence, changes in the availability of funds *may* be as important as, or even more important than, changes in the interest rate.

In the late 1940's and early 1950's some economists used this fact to develop the so-called "availability doctrine" to show how monetary policy could discourage investment even if only relatively small changes in the interest rate were permitted. This availability theory does not consist of a single result worked out in great detail but rather is a conglomeration of related effects. They are: (1) the portfolio effect, (2) the locking-in effect, (3) the yield differential effect, (4) the investment banking effect, and (5) the expectations effect.

The *portfolio effect* works as follows. A rise in interest rates reduces the value of outstanding securities and thus reduces the public's liquidity.[6] And since the

---

[6] A rise in interest rates *reduces* the price of outstanding securities. The increase in interest rates does not apply to outstanding, i.e., previously issued, securities, and these old securities now have to compete with new securities paying a higher rate of interest; hence their price has to fall. To illustrate, consider the case of a "consol," that is, a security on which the issuer pays interest every year but that has no maturity date on which it has to be paid off. (At present, such securities do not exist in the United States, but in Britain the government has issued such securities.) Suppose that a consol pays an interest rate of 3 percent, and that the rate of interest now rises to 6 percent. The owner of the old consol still gets only $30 on each $1000 bond outstanding. If he sells his $1000 bond for $500 the buyer purchasing two of these bonds for his $1000 would get exactly the same return

public is holding a very large volume of securities, even a small change in the rate of interest has a substantial effect. According to the proponents of the availability approach, this reduction in liquidity reduces investment in two ways. First, borrowers are less willing to invest as the value of their liquid assets declines. A simple equilibrium model suffices to show this. Assume that the firm or household possesses liquid assets and physical capital. Now, reduce its liquid assets; unless they are an inferior good the unit will react by partially restoring its stock of liquid assets at the expense of its stock of physical capital. (By analogy, consider a consumer who has apples and pears. If you take away some of his apples, he will reach an equilibrium only by swapping some pears against apples.)

The second way in which a reduction in wealth and liquidity reduces investment is through its impact on lenders. As the lender's liquidity is reduced by falling security prices, he becomes less willing to reduce it even further by exchanging liquid government securities for less liquid private securities or loans. The institutional framework of this argument is that in a period of tight money financial institutions can meet rising private demands for credit only by selling gov-

---

as he would by buying one new bond at $1000. Hence, to keep old securities competitive with new securities, the price of old securities has to fall by half as the interest rate doubles. This inversely *proportional* relationship applies only to consols; for securities with a fixed maturity the price still moves inversely to the interest rate but no longer does so proportionately. If a bond is redeemable in, say, five years, the purchaser receives the old (lower) rate of interest only for five years; after that he gets his $1000 back and is able to invest that sum in the higher yielding bonds. Hence, although doubling the interest rate still reduces bond prices it does not cut them in half. The shorter the period until the maturity of the security, the less is the effect of a change in interest rates on its capital value.

ernment securities. But banks, savings and loan associations, and other financial intermediaries hold government securities not only for earnings but also to ensure their liquidity. Hence, a reduction in the value of the liquidity stock of these financial institutions makes them less willing to reduce it even further by selling government securities. Conversely, during a period of falling interest rates and rising security prices, financial institutions find the liquidity of their portfolios increasing, and so they tend to restore these portfolios to equilibrium by selling government securities and making loans or purchasing private securities.

The second argument of the availability approach is the locking-in effect. This effect, too, relies on the fall in value of securities as interest rates rise, but, unlike the portfolio effect just discussed, it relies primarily, not on rational profit maximization, but on an irrationality. According to the availability doctrine, portfolio managers have an aversion to selling securities at a loss, even if they could more than recoup these losses by using the proceeds of the security sales to make high yielding loans. If these managers sell securities at a loss this loss shows up on their balance sheets, while the higher yield they obtain on private loans does not show up directly on their current balance sheets. (For accounting purposes banks may value their government security portfolios at cost; if they hold on to their government securities as prices fall the price decline does not show up on their balance sheet.) Hence, portfolio managers may be criticized by their superiors and by stockholders if they sell securities at a loss even if this action increases the long-run profits of the firm.[7] Conversely, during

[7] Note that the irrationality that comes into play in this locking-in effect is not necessarily on the part of the financial manager; he may maximize his salary by not selling securities even if

a recession when interest rates have fallen and security prices have risen portfolio managers can gain prestige by selling securities and making lower yielding private loans.

The third aspect of the availability thesis is the *yield differential effect.* This argument relies on the stickiness of interest rates on private loans and securities. It asserts that as interest rates rise on government securities, interest rates on private loans and securities increase, too, but do so only with a substantial lag. Hence, for a significant period of time government securities have a competitive advantage over private securities and loans, and banks and other lenders will tend to hold on to their government securities. Conversely, during a recession a reduction in the interest rate on government securities makes lenders more willing to sell government securities and invest in private ventures, thus raising investment and income.

A fourth aspect of the availability thesis raised by its proponents is the *investment banking effect.* The investment banker usually floats securities in the following manner. He obtains the securities from the original issuer, paying a fixed price for the issue, and then sells the securities for whatever he can get on the fluctuating market. If interest rates rise while he is holding them he may sustain a loss on the transaction, but if interest rates fall and security prices rise he will make a substantial profit. Hence, the argument runs, during a period of rising interest rates investment bankers tend to be unwilling to float securi-

---

this failure to sell securities reduces the income of the firm. Rather, the irrationality here is that the firm does not fire him.

Moreover, there is an aspect of the locking-in effect which is rational for the bank. Some regulations limit certain types of assets to a fixed proportion of the bank's capital. By not selling securities at a loss the bank maintains the book value of its capital and the amount of these assets it can hold.

ties, and this retards investment spending. By contrast, in a period of falling interest rates investment bankers are more willing to float securities and facilitate investment.

Thus we are left with the *expectations* effect, one of the biggest and most controversial aspects of the availability doctrine. The argument has several facets. On the one hand, the argument states, if interest rates rise, lenders expect them to rise even further. Hence, they reduce their lending and their security purchases while waiting for the rates to rise. It is not actually necessary that lenders have strong expectations that rates will rise; the mere creation of *uncertainty* about the possibility that rates may rise is sufficient. (This fact illustrates the workings of Keynes' speculative motive for liquidity preference.) On the other hand, borrowers have different expectations; as rates rise they expect rates to fall again and hence postpone borrowing and investing. Thus, both the supply curve and the demand curve for funds shift leftwards, and investment is reduced.

Moreover, these effects on lenders and borrowers are supplemented by more general effects on investors, particularly investors in inventories. As interest rates rise, investors realize that the Federal Reserve is stepping in to control inflation and that there is now less need to buy ahead to protect against future price increases. Conversely, in a recession, as the Federal Reserve takes expansionary action businessmen feel more optimistic and hence are less prone to cut back on investment.

This availability thesis has been criticized by a number of economists on several grounds. First, even if one grants that all of the effects described above work in the direction indicated, how strong are they? In arguing that a monetary policy is strong one cannot merely point out that it has some effects on investment; one must show that these effects are powerful. Unfortunately, both the supporters and the critics of the availability thesis have little real evidence to offer. Second, the whole approach is based on market imperfections and at least in part on irrationality. While such behavior may be operative for a while, it is likely to decrease over time. In this connection it is worth noting that the assumptions about behavior reflected in the availability doctrine were more likely to have been valid in the 1950's than now. In the 1950's, when the pegging of interest rates was finally abandoned, the financial community was unfamiliar with a flexible monetary policy and hence was more likely to have suffered from a locking-in effect than now when it is again familiar with fluctuating security prices.

To move on to some more specific criticisms, first, the locking-in effect is weakened in that financial institutions need not sell long-term government securities to make loans but can sell short-term securities instead, and on short-term securities the capital loss is quite minor. Second, a technical quirk in our tax laws at times gives banks an incentive to sell securities at a loss, which tends to make the locking-in effect work perversely. Finally, there have been some studies of the locking-in effects—with mixed results. In any case, an additional factor has recently entered the picture. Banks have to pledge government securities as collateral for government (federal, state, and local) deposits. As a result many banks currently have few government securities they could sell, so that for banks the locking-in effect is both less important and less necessary now than in the past.

The yield differential effect can provide only temporary help to monetary policy. Once yields on private securities adjust to the higher yields on government securities this effect disappears.

As for the investment banking effect, the impact of tight money on these bankers also tends to wear off after some time.

Most criticism of the availability doctrine has centered on the expectations effect. There is indeed little reason to assume that expectations are as convenient a *deus ex machina* as the availability doctrine assumes. Why should lenders expect rates to continue to rise and borrowers expect them to fall? The opposite set of expectations would be just as plausible. In any case, the assumption that borrowers and lenders have different expectations is most questionable.[8] Similarly, businessmen's expectations in general need not follow as convenient a pattern as the availability doctrine assumes. If the Federal Reserve adopts a tight money policy, businessmen may interpret this not as a signal that inflation is stopping but that inflation is a severe danger. Conversely, an easy money policy may be read not as a hopeful sign but as an indication of a recession.

Thus the availability doctrine is open to criticism by those who are skeptical as to its strength.

All in all these criticisms suggest that the availability effect is not as strong as its originators thought. But, on the other hand, most economists would prob-

[8] To be sure, one could argue that, in a period of tight money, investment will be inhibited even if both lenders and borrowers assume that interest rates will rise further. In this case lenders will have an incentive to hold off lending. Although borrowers have an incentive to speed up their borrowing, there is little reason why they should use the borrowed funds for physical investment right away. Thus the expectations of the lenders tend to reduce investment while borrowers' expectations have no effect on investment so that the net effect is a reduction in investment.

ably not be willing to dismiss it completely by any means. In spite of the above criticisms there does seem to be *something* to the availability effect.

Some Factors Limiting the Strength of Monetary Policy

Having discussed the availability doctrine, let us look at the other side of the picture—at some factors weakening the impact of Federal Reserve monetary policy.

Although, as the availability thesis shows, a large, widely held government debt tends in some ways to strengthen monetary policy, there are also ways in which it weakens monetary policy.[9] First, a large, widely distributed public debt facilitates the mobilization of idle funds throughout the economy. Turning idle balances into active balances raises velocity and, hence, allows the same quantity of money to finance a larger volume of expenditures. Federal Reserve attempts to control aggregate expenditures by controlling the quantity of money are therefore frustrated by offsetting changes in velocity.

A large, widely held public debt facilitates the activation of idle bank balances by providing prospective spenders with liquid assets that they can easily sell to holders of idle money balances. For example, as customers request more loans, commercial banks can sell securities. As holders of idle balances purchase these securities from banks, their individual bank deposits are reduced. But since bank reserves have not fallen, banks can create new deposits by making loans.

[9] For an outstanding exposition of this point of view, see Warren L. Smith, "On the Effectiveness of Monetary Policy," *American Economic Review*, Vol. 46 (September, 1956), pp. 588–606.

In this way deposits are transferred from one group of customers (who bought the securities) to another group (who obtained bank loans). People who buy securities from banks when rising interest rates make it more profitable to hold these securities are likely to have relatively idle balances—if these people had intended to spend their funds on goods and services they would be unlikely to buy securities instead. On the other hand, customers who borrow from banks probably spend these funds since generally people do not borrow to hold idle balances. Thus, velocity and, hence, expenditures are increased by this transfer of deposits. This process of activating idle balances is not confined to banks; other financial institutions like savings and loan associations and life insurance companies may sell securities and lend the proceeds to prospective spenders.

Furthermore, the widespread holding of the public debt can activate idle bank balances directly without the help of financial intermediaries. Corporations or households wishing to spend can sell their government securities on the open market to holders of idle balances. In all of these ways velocity is increased, and expenditures can thus rise in spite of the Federal Reserve's tight money policy. Conversely, in a period of easy money interest rates fall, and the public has less incentive to buy securities from banks and from potential spenders. Hence, there is a decline in velocity which tends to offset the increase in the money stock brought about by an easy money policy. In both easy and tight money policies, changes in the interest rate induce changes in velocity that partially offset the effect of changes in the quantity of money. (Put into Keynesian language, the argument runs as follows: the liquidity preference schedule is interest elastic and the marginal efficiency of investment schedule is interest

inelastic. Hence, changes in the quantity of money
have but a limited effect on the interest rate, and the
interest rate, in turn, has little effect on investment.)

Many economists who believe that monetary policy
is powerful would agree that, in principle, the factors
just described weaken monetary policy, but they
would argue that the size of these effects is rather
minor. In recent years the ratio of bank loans to deposits has risen very substantially. It is uncertain how
much further banks would allow loans to rise in a
period of tight money. In addition, as previously
mentioned, banks have pledged a substantial proportion of their government securities as collateral for
government deposits, and this limits their ability to
increase velocity by selling securities. But note that
these points apply only to banks and not to other
financial institutions.

A second point raised by economists who are skeptical about a tight money policy is that tight money
changes the structure of the money market; as interest
rates rise, innovations occur in the money market that
allow the participants to carry on their activities with
a smaller ratio of money to sales or to income.[10] Not
only do these innovations counteract the effects of a
tight money policy, but later on when money is eased
these innovations do not disappear; they become a
permanent feature of the money market. As a result,
periods of tight money induce a long run decline in
the ratio of money to income and to debt. When this
lower ratio of money to income and debt is combined
with the effects of the banking systems' selling government securities that are then replaced by private secu-

[10] See Hyman Minsky, "Central Banking and Money Market
Changes," *Quarterly Journal of Economics,* Vol. 71 (May,
1957), pp. 171–187. For a description of some of the devices
used, see also "The Scramble for Money," *Business Week,*
Special Report (November 17, 1956), pp. 64–106.

rities, the money market becomes more and more vulnerable to shocks. As Hyman Minsky, the leading proponent of this view, has put it:[11]

> . . . every institutional innovation which results in both new ways to finance business and new substitutes for cash assets decreases the liquidity of the economy. That is, even though the amount of money does not change, the liquidity of the community decreases when government debt is replaced by private debt in the portfolios of commercial banks. Also when nonfinancial corporations replace cash with government bonds and then government bonds with debts of bond houses, liquidity decreases. Such a pyramiding of liquid assets implies that the risks to the economy increase, for insolvency or even temporary illiquidity of a key nonbank organization can have a chain reaction, and affect the solvency or liquidity of many organizations. . . . the effort by the central bank to control inflation abets the development of unstable conditions in the money market. . . .

Again, defenders of monetary policy would raise the question of how strong these effects actually are. That statistical demand functions for money (which are based on the assumption that there are no such irreversibilities) get good fits suggests that these irreversibilities *may* not be very significant. Moreover, the argument runs, institutional changes since 1929 have made our financial system panic-proof.

In addition to these changes, economists who believe that monetary policy is weak have often pointed to a third factor: the influence of nonbank financial intermediaries.[12] The operations of nonbank financial

[11] Minsky, *op. cit.,* pp. 184 and 187.

[12] The leading advocates of this approach are John Gurley and Edward Shaw. For a brief statement, see their "Financial Aspects of Economic Development," *American Economic Review,* Vol. 45 (September, 1955), pp. 515–538. In Britain this view has been strongly championed by the Committee

intermediaries may be destabilizing both in the short run and the long run. In the short run, during an expansion as interest rates rise generally throughout the economy, the opportunity cost of holding demand deposits rises, and the public has an incentive to switch out of demand deposits and hold deposits of nonbank financial intermediaries instead. The financial intermediary holds its funds either as a deposit with a commercial bank or else buys securities from, or makes loans to, someone who deposits the receipts in a commercial bank. In either case, commercial bank deposits are not reduced by this shift of bank customers to, for example, a savings and loan association except to the trivial extent that the savings and loan holds currency. All that happens is that instead of the original depositor holding a deposit in the commercial bank the savings and loan association (or someone who received the funds from it) now holds the deposit. There has been pyramiding of financial assets; the total of bank deposits *plus* savings and loan deposits has increased. If expenditures depend in part upon the total stock of liquid assets rather than merely upon the quantity of money, this development is inflationary.

But recent experience shows little evidence of such a danger. It is true that demand deposits, as a percent of deposits in major depository intermediaries, have declined since the end of the war while at the same time interest rates have been rising. However, this correlation has been one of secular movement only; cyclical changes in the bill rate have not been reflected in a decline of the demand deposit ratio. This fact is not surprising. The rates paid by depository institutions change only with a lag as the money market changes.

---

on the Workings of the Monetary System, usually called the Radcliff Committee.

Moreover, there is probably a lag in the response of depositors to higher rates paid by these intermediaries. In addition, once a firm or household has decided to switch its deposit to a savings and loan association, it probably does not switch back to a commercial bank if the interest rate paid by the savings and loan association declines. Hence, there is little danger of cyclical swings between demand deposits and other types of deposits offsetting Federal Reserve policy. Conceivably, such a danger might arise in the future but there is no such indication from past data.

In addition to having a potential for cyclical destabilization, nonbank financial intermediaries may also create another, long-range problem. Demand deposits as a percent of the public's total liquid asset holdings have been declining over time. According to the general liquidity approach, a monetary theory discussed a great deal in recent years, aggregate demand depends not upon the quantity of money per se but upon the total of liquid assets or, indeed, of any debt. According to this view, liquid assets are easily turned into cash and, hence, provide the wherewithal for expenditures. Thus, during an expansion the public can raise expenditures by running down its nonmoney liquid assets.

If this theory is valid the secular decline in the share of demand deposits as a proportion of total liquid assets may create a serious problem for monetary policy. If the Federal Reserve limits the growth of demand deposits in an economy in which other liquid assets are rising rapidly, the importance of demand deposits will decline further and further. As put by John Gurley:

> Can the relationships among the sluggish growth of money, the relatively rapid expansion of other financial assets and the traditional base for monetary controls be

purely accidental? No. The expansion of other highly liquid assets, at times so rapid as to threaten the stability of the economy, prompted the monetary authorities to clamp down on the one asset they could directly control—the money supply. The screws were tightened on commercial banks and the money supply to compensate for increasing liquidity elsewhere. Moreover, when borrowers were blocked at the doors of commercial banks, they turned to other financial institutions, and this added pressure stimulated the growth of these institutions. The result has been a diminishing role for money in the liquidity pool, and a relatively declining role for commercial banks within the family of private financial institutions. . . .[13]

If the general liquidity approach is correct and the quantity of money matters only insofar as it is part of total liquid assets, the decline in the share of demand deposits means that to get a given effect on expenditures the Federal Reserve will have to change the quantity of money by a greater and greater proportion all the time.[14] Since very large changes in the volume of demand deposits may prove disruptive to the economy, the Federal Reserve is, in this way, losing control over the economy. Hence, it may be necessary either to impose controls over nonbank financial intermediaries or else to reduce controls over commercial banks so that they are able to compete better with their more freewheeling competitors.

[13] Testimony before the Joint Economic Committee, *Review of the Report of the Commission on Money and Credit, Hearings* (Washington, D.C.: 79th Congress, First Session, 1961), p. 285.

[14] This reasoning assumes that the changes in the money stock do not lead to corresponding, roughly proportional changes in the stock of nonmoney liquid assets. This is a debatable issue. For a good discussion of this type of problem, see Donald Shelby, "Some Implications of the Growth of Financial Intermediaries," *Journal of Finance*, Vol. 13 (December, 1958), pp. 527–541.

But there are qualifications to this view. First and most fundamentally, there is the question whether the liquidity approach is correct. If, as the quantity theory claims, what matters is the quantity of money rather than the stock of liquid assets, then the growth of non-money liquid assets is irrelevant. The fact that a number of empirical studies have found stable demand functions for money for the postwar period when non-money liquid assets were growing rapidly suggests that the growth of these assets may not have made the relation between money and income more unstable.

The second qualification is that the declining trend in the share of bank deposits among total liquid assets may come to a stop before it has gone very much further. In any case, to some extent the government has already started to impose controls over nonbank intermediaries. Under temporary legislation passed in 1966, the federal government can impose—and currently has in force—a ceiling on interest rates paid by savings and loan associations and savings banks. In addition, a quite simple change in regulations, a change advocated in any case by many economists for other reasons, may put a limit to the decline in the role of demand deposits. This change would be to permit banks to pay interest on demand deposits so that the public has less of an incentive to economize on the use of demand deposits.

Before leaving the subject of financial intermediaries we should note that in addition to the professional financial intermediaries, monetary policy also has to contend with what might be called amateur financial intermediaries. In a tight money period firms, particularly large firms, extend trade credit to their customers. This credit extension may allow a larger volume of transactions with a given money stock and, hence, by raising the income velocity of money can have an inflationary potential.

The Relationship of Strength and Magnitude

There is one line of thought that suggests that regardless of any of the qualifications discussed above, monetary policy is always strong enough to do the job. If a given change in the reserve base does not suffice to change income enough, all the monetary authorities would have to do is to change the reserve base by greater and greater amounts and eventually income would change to the desired extent. If variations in velocity offset much of the effect of changes in the quantity of money, this merely means that a substantial change in the money stock is required to do what a small change would do if velocity were stable. Since the Federal Reserve *can* change the money stock substantially, one can argue that the offsetting changes in velocity do not really matter. In fact, Lawrence Ritter has argued that changes in velocity facilitate monetary policy by providing a safety valve. If the Federal Reserve tightens money too abruptly velocity increases and the Federal Reserve can modify its policy before it causes significant damage.[15]

The view that a tight money policy, if carried far enough, could choke off a boom has been accepted for many years, but for a long time many economists argued that the power of monetary policy is asymmetrical. If money is made tight enough it can end the boom, but however far an easy money policy is carried it cannot stop a depression. As two popular

[15] Lawrence Ritter, "Income-Velocity and Anti-Inflationary Monetary Policy," *American Economic Review*, Vol. 49 (March, 1959), pp. 120–129.

clichés have it, "You can't push on a piece of string" and "You can lead a horse to water, but you can't make it drink." This viewpoint (which is based in good part on the standard Keynesian interpretation of the Great Depression) has been severely challenged in recent years, and the belief in the asymmetry of monetary policy has lost much of its support.[16]

This approach to monetary policy (claiming that a monetary policy strong enough to do the job always exists) is extremely important; if it is correct, the whole problem of the strength of monetary policy is irrelevant. All that is required is that the Federal Reserve have the courage of its convictions and initiate very substantial changes in the money stock. It is therefore worth seeing if there are any qualifications of this view.

One qualification is that the change in velocity may not be accurately predictable. If so, the monetary policy adopted may turn out to be either too strong or too weak. To be sure, in either case follow-up action could be used to correct the error, but such a delayed response would lengthen the lags of monetary policy and thus might create instability. Given the Federal Reserve's great uncertainty both about underlying conditions and about the impact of its own policies, it is very hard for the Federal Reserve to proceed in any but small steps.

A second difficulty with the idea of simply reducing bank reserves until the desired change in aggregate demand occurs is that a sharp rise in interest rates might disrupt financial markets. For example, the 1967 Report of the Council of Economic Advisers expressed the belief that in August, 1966 "monetary policy was probably as tight as it could get without

[16] See Harry Johnson, "Monetary Theory and Policy," *American Economic Review*, Vol. 52 (June, 1962), p. 366.

risking financial disorder." [17] At first glance this reasoning seems fallacious. The very purpose of a tight money policy is to cut back investment. Hence, to say that a very large increase in interest rates reduces investment too much is to leave oneself open to rejoinder that if a small increase in interest rates does not do enough, and a very large increase is much too powerful, there must be some intermediate increase which is just right. The only answer to this argument is that this optimal intermediate increase is too hard to determine and that the penalty for overshooting the mark is too great to take the risk. But this argument is really nothing but a special case of the previously discussed point about uncertainty.

A third objection to the view that a tight money policy can be pressed as far as needs be is its interference with public debt management. With the large proportion of the public debt that is in the form of short-term securities, the Treasury frequently undertakes substantial refinancing operations. To help the Treasury in placing this debt, the Federal Reserve refrains from tightening money at a time the Treasury is refinancing and tries to keep security markets "on an even keel." This need to help the Treasury hinders the maintenance of a powerful, tight money policy. Note, however, that this problem would not arise if the Treasury would keep a much smaller portion of the debt in short-term form or would worry less about an unsuccessful refinancing operation. But even then a substantial rise in interest rates would be expensive for the Treasury, the country's biggest debtor.

Fourth, a very sharp, tight money policy would cause some reallocation of resources and some redis-

[17] *Economic Report of the President* (Washington, D.C.: Executive Office of the President, 1967), p. 60.

tribution of income (matters discussed in Chapter 4), which many people would consider undesirable.

Fifth, there is the danger that sharp increases in the interest rate would cause the financial community to innovate new methods of economizing on cash balances, so that over a period of time, velocity would tend to rise substantially. As Minsky has emphasized, a high ratio of credit to final means of payment and to income flows creates a danger of a financial collapse during a cyclical downturn.

All of these arguments refer to pushing a tight money policy very far and, with the exception of the first one dealing with uncertainty, are not really objections to a very strong *easy* money policy. There is, however, one objection to a very aggressive easy money policy. As Federal Reserve Chairman Martin has frequently said, a powerful easy money policy creates a large amount of liquidity for banks and for the economy in general. When economic conditions change and warrant a tight money policy a long time is required until the Federal Reserve can mop up this excess liquidity. This delays the "bite" of a tight money policy too long.

How important are these qualifications? Again, there is no unanimity on this question. The great majority of economists would probably agree that there is enough substance to these qualifications so that one cannot simply settle the question of the strength of monetary policy by saying that the Federal Reserve should adopt so radical a policy that it can get any effect it wants. On the other hand, the possibility of inducing greater changes in the reserve base than have been usual in the past does reinforce the conclusion suggested in the previous section that monetary policy can have a substantial effect on income. One factor supporting this conclusion is that in recent years there has been great improvement in the Federal Reserve's research on monetary policy. As economists obtain more knowledge of how monetary policy operates, the Federal Reserve will be able to use stronger policies with less fear of making a mistake.

International Aspects

So far this chapter has dealt only with the power of monetary policy to achieve its domestic goals. But in addition to this task, monetary policy also plays a role in obtaining balance-of-payments equilibrium. It does so in two ways. First, an increase in money income, whether due to price rises or output increases, raises the demand for imports and tends to move the balance of payments in a deficit direction; a reduction in money income does the opposite. Thus by influencing the level of money income the Federal Reserve is able to help achieve balance-of-payments equilibrium. Second, monetary policy affects the balance of payments by changing interest rates.

If foreigners invest in United States securities or deposits, this generates a demand for dollars and, therefore, is a positive item on the United States balance of payments.[18] Conversely, if United States residents purchase foreign securities or undertake direct investment in a foreign country, these kinds of transactions enter the balance of payments as a negative item. Now, the decision to invest in one country rather than in another is made, in part, on the basis of the

[18] This statement needs qualification. The Department of Commerce computes the United States balance of payments in two different ways. One way does not count short-term foreign investment in the United States as a positive item; the other way does.

relative interest rates ruling in different countries. Hence, by changing interest rates, the central bank can affect the balance of payments.

The size of the effect that can be achieved by relatively small changes in the interest rate on foreign investment is still undetermined. Again, one could argue that since a *substantial* rise in interest rates would attract large amounts of foreign funds (as well as limit capital outflows), monetary policy is powerful enough. But there are several qualifications to this optimistic view.

First, as pointed out in Chapter 1, there is a potential conflict among goals. Balance-of-payments equilibrium may be incompatible with full employment, adequate growth, and even with price stability. Although a higher interest rate may ameliorate the balance-of-payments problem it may make the unemployment problem worse.

One method that has been used to reduce this conflict is to play on the structure of interest rates. The foreign investment that is most easily influenced by central bank manipulation of the interest rate is short-term investment. Hence, if the central bank can raise the short-term rate without raising the long- and intermediate-term rates, it may succeed in helping the balance of payments without seriously hindering the achievement of full employment. This policy of twisting the yield curve (called "operation twist") has been tried by the United States in recent years. Note that the feasibility of this operation depends upon the assumption that Federal Reserve and Treasury operations are powerful enough to twist the yield curve, an assumption which is open to question. In addition, the success of this policy depends upon investment being substantially more sensitive to the long- and intermediate-term interest rates than to the short-term rate. While this view has widespread support there is little firm evidence on this subject.

Another difficulty with raising interest rates to cure a balance-of-payments deficit is that high interest rates, by reducing domestic income, may make long-term domestic investment less profitable and in this way may stimulate foreign investment. If income is depressed in the United States, corporations may prefer to use their limited funds to build plants in more buoyant markets abroad rather than in the United States. Moreover, United States commodity exports are influenced by the degree of technological innovation in our economy. By retarding domestic investment, tight money may conceivably make the balance-of-payments problem worse in the long run. It is hard to know how important these offsetting factors are—but it is doubtful that they should be dismissed out of hand.

In any case, high interest rates are no cure for a *long-run* balance-of-payments problem. Although an inflow of foreign funds helps the balance of payments while it occurs, the subsequent interest payments on these funds make the balance-of-payments deficit worse. And the same thing applies to a reduction in United States foreign investment, which reduces future inflows of interest and dividends.

Finally, there is a danger that foreign central banks would match rising interest rates in the United States by raising *their* interest rates. The extent to which this is a real danger will vary from time to time depending upon the balance-of-payments pressures felt by other countries.

Chapter 4 | The Efficiency of Monetary Policy

Suppose that it were shown conclusively that monetary policy is strong. This fact alone would not suffice to make monetary policy a useful stabilization tool. A strong but inefficient monetary policy may do more harm than good. Moreover, most economists would argue that fiscal policy can also be strong enough. In choosing between the two, and indeed in deciding whether to use either one, it is necessary to assess their efficiencies. The efficiency of a stabilization policy must be judged by two criteria: its timing and its effect on resource allocation. Let us look at each of these in turn.

The Problem of Lags

The issue is by no means settled whether countercyclical monetary policy, as presently conducted, stabilizes or destabilizes the economy. To be stabilizing a policy must have its *expansionary effects* at a time when income is low and its *restrictive effects* when income is high. *Adopting* an expansionary policy in a period of low income and a restrictive policy in a period of high income *may* destabilize the economy if there are long lags between the adoption of a policy and its effects on income. Suppose that as inflationary conditions develop, the Federal Reserve reduced bank reserves. *If* this action cuts aggregate demand only after a long lag, the fall in aggregate demand may take place only after the economy has passed the cyclical turning point and is in a recession. During this recession the central bank may reverse itself and adopt an expansionary policy. But *if* this policy, too, takes a long time to affect income, then it *may* serve not to ameliorate the recession but may reinforce the inflation during the subsequent expansion. Thus, as is shown in Figure 2, a countercyclical policy *may* have procyclical effects. Good intentions are not enough. In fact, it can be shown that to have a net stabilizing effect, the policy must do the right thing *more* than half the time.[1] If the timing of policy is not quite good, a strong policy is worse than a weak one and may be destabilizing rather than stabilizing.

The important empirical question here is: How long does it take monetary policy to have its effects on income? Does a policy adopted in one stage of the cycle have its main impact on income only after the turning point?[2] Unfortunately, there is still considerable disagreement among economists about how long it takes monetary policy to affect income. Such economists as

[1] See Milton Friedman, "The Effects of a Full Employment Policy on Economic Stabilization: A Formal Analysis," in his *Essays in Positive Economics* (Chicago: University of Chicago Press, 1953), pp. 117–132.

[2] It is tempting to argue that, in this case, all the Federal Reserve has to do is to base its policy on a forecast and adopt a tight money policy in a recession and an easy money policy in an upswing. But there are two difficulties with this suggestion. First, the ability to forecast business conditions may not be sufficient for this, and second, the lags may, as Friedman thinks, vary a great deal in an unpredictable way from case to case.

Milton Friedman think that monetary policy is usually very slow to affect income. Other economists, like John Culbertson, think the effects of monetary policy are quickly felt. A number of detailed studies of this issue have been undertaken, and, although they differed substantially in their conclusions, only a single one

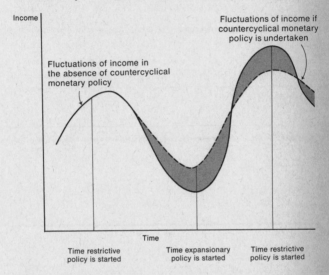

Figure 2. Possible Effect of Stabilization Policy on Economic Fluctuations.

NOTE: Shaded areas denote changes in income induced by monetary policy.

argued that the lag was less than half a year—and many of these studies found a much longer lag than that.[3] Hence, although these studies have been subjected to some criticisms, there is room for legitimate doubt whether monetary policy can really ameliorate the business cycle.

[3] For a summary of the numerous studies, see my *Monetary Policy in the United States* (New York: Random House, in preparation), Appendix to Chapter 6.

Monetary Policy and Resource Allocation

Let us now look at the second aspect of efficiency: resource allocation. One of the main claims in favor of monetary policy is that it does not interfere with resource allocation, that it changes aggregate demand in a neutral manner so that there are no unfavorable side effects. By contrast, the argument runs, fiscal policy impinges on specific sectors of the economy (e.g., a public works program) or on specific income groups (e.g., tax reductions). In doing so it interferes with the resource allocation and income distribution patterns resulting from the interplay of free-market factors.

Economists who are critical of this line of argument have taken either one of two stands. Either they have argued that monetary policy is in fact *not* neutral, or else they have argued that neutrality is not "a good thing."

To evaluate both of these arguments one must clarify the meaning of neutrality. One possible interpretation is that neutrality means having a proportional effect on all sectors of the economy. For example, if a tight money policy cuts aggregate demand by, say, 3 percent, all types of investment as well as consumption are reduced by 3 percent. If one uses this definition of neutrality, the problem is very simple; monetary policy is far from neutral—different types of investment are affected differently. But this interpretation of neutrality as a proportionality misses the point completely. Proportional change in all sectors of the economy is *not* an adequate criterion for choosing policy. Proportionality would generally be inconsistent with optimal resource allocation.

An adequate definition of neutrality requires a more sophisticated treatment. Neutrality must be interpreted as letting the free market decide where to increase or reduce demand. And generally the free market would *not* decide to increase or to reduce demand proportionately in all sectors, any more than a household experiencing a doubling of income would decide to double its expenditures on each and every commodity. Consider, for example, a tight money policy instituted in an inflationary environment. Aggregate demand is too high, and the Federal Reserve now brings about an increase in the interest rate. The increase in the interest rate means that the cost of using resources either for current consumption or for investment has increased. This operates as a signal to the economy to reduce its demand. Households cut back on consumption until the marginal loss from postponing consumption from this year to the next is equal to the interest rate, and firms similarly reduce investment until the rate of return on investment is once again equal to the interest rate. If one can take the distribution of income as optimal (or as exogenously given) and if the other welfare conditions are met, the reduction in aggregate demand occurs where it involved the least loss of utility to the economy.[4]

Contrast this with fiscal policy. Suppose that government expenditures are cut to curb inflation. If one assumes for illustration that the equilibrium value of the multiplier is two, half the reduction in aggregate demand occurs within the governmental sector. If the public were given a choice where to cut its expenditures, it is unlikely that it would decide to con-

[4] As usual in applied economics, the difficulties of constructing a social welfare function are handled in the most convenient way—by simply ignoring them.

centrate half the cut in one category: government services. A somewhat similar criticism applies to the other side of fiscal policy: changes in tax rates. Here, a tax cut gives the public more disposable income to allocate in an optimizing manner, but there is still an interference with income distribution since the tax cut usually affects different income groups differently. Unlike monetary policy, fiscal policy is not neutral— it substitutes the decisions of government officials for the decisions of the free market.

This line of reasoning has been criticized on two grounds. Some economists have argued that neutrality as defined above is *not* desirable, and some, while accepting neutrality as desirable, have argued that monetary policy is not really neutral.

Note that a neutral monetary policy does not cure existing maladjustments and distortions in the economy—it leaves them unaffected. In principle, it is possible to analyze the effect of monetary policy on resource allocation without worrying about misallocations that exist independently of monetary policy. But in many discussions this distinction becomes blurred. People who are very concerned about a particular resource allocation problem want stabilization policy to help solve this problem. Thus a stabilization policy that is merely neutral vis-à-vis this problem seems inferior to one that ameliorates this particular resource allocation problem. Hence, in popular arguments both lines of criticism tend to merge. But for analysis one must separate them; so let us start with the argument that neutrality as defined above (p. 97) is not desirable.

The argument that a neutral monetary policy is undesirable is based on the following consideration. Neutrality is desirable only if all the conditions for welfare maximization in a free enterprise system are met.[5] If they are not met, fiscal policy (or any other policy) that is *not* neutral *may* increase welfare. The fact that monetary policy does not interfere with a nonoptimal situation is not necessarily a point in its favor. For example, a number of economists believe, rightly or wrongly, that a free-market system saves too small a proportion of its income. Let us assume, for the sake of argument, that this is correct. If so, the fact that a tight money policy brings about a proportionately greater reduction in investment than in consumption is a drawback of this policy even if such an allocation of resources corresponds to the free choice of the participants in the market place. Similarly, if the distribution of income is not optimal, changes in tax rates, though they interfere with the free-market system, *may* increase economic well-being.

Clearly the conditions necessary for optimal resource allocation in a free market are not met fully in practice, and one may therefore be tempted to argue that the neutrality of monetary policy is a "bad thing." But this conclusion does not necessarily follow. Although resource allocation and income distribution are not optimal, a policy that is not neutral *could* make resource allocation and income distribution worse than they otherwise would be, instead of better. Some of the provisions of our tax laws surely distort rather than improve resource allocation. The best case for a free market, that is, for conservative economic policy, is not that in the absence of government interference everyone would live in a perfect world but rather that government interference often makes a situation, which admittedly is not ideal to start with,

[5] These conditions are an optimal distribution of income, full employment, perfect competition in all markets, and no uncompensated external economies or diseconomies.

still worse. Thus one's reaction to the neutrality of monetary policy really involves one's political views. Liberals, who take the shortcomings of a free-market system seriously and have faith in governmental policy, tend to favor fiscal policy because they believe that the government is efficient enough to ameliorate the shortcomings of a free market. Conservatives believe the opposite. Clearly, the issue of the relative efficiency of governmental policies and the free market transcends the topic of monetary policy and, hence, is not discussed here.

Now let us look at the other line of criticism that asserts that monetary policy is *not* neutral. This criticism relies upon the fact that there are many imperfections in the capital market so that the interest rate does not serve as an efficient signal.[6]

One important imperfection in the money market is existence of credit rationing already discussed in the previous chapter. To a considerable extent banks do not allocate their funds to the highest bidder, but instead they ration credit among their customers. This means that the interest rate does not serve as an allocating device. While a rise in the rate of interest serves to cut back investment where its yield is least, credit rationing does not necessarily do this. Hence, the argument runs, monetary policy does not further the optimal allocation of resources. The decision where to cut investment is made, not by an impersonal market, but by bankers. Like fiscal policy, monetary policy, the argument goes, involves "the rule of men" rather than the rule of impersonal economic forces. To be sure, one could counter this argument by saying that

---

[6] In a way this second line of criticism is merely a special case of the first type of criticism since it relies on the fact that one of the conditions of economic welfare, perfect competition in the capital market, is not met.

the rule of men involved in monetary policy is that of a large number of widely dispersed individuals, whereas in the case of fiscal policy the men who do the ruling are a small number of politicians and bureaucrats. But, one could turn this latter argument around and say that decisions are better made by democratically elected officials than by an oligarchy of bankers. But we will end this discussion before it intrudes on political issues.

It is worth noting, however, that capital rationing by banks is not the only imperfection of the capital market. Small business has only limited access to the capital market, so that capital is not perfectly allocated between large and small business. Morever, many interest rates are sticky and do not reflect the movements of the more sensitive rates. For example, in the early stages of a tight money policy, when interest rates paid by depository institutions have not yet risen, the signal to reduce aggregate demand has not yet reached households. Similarly, the locking-in effect, as well as some of the other factors stressed by the availability doctrine, illustrate the existence of various money market imperfections that distort resource allocation.

The frequent claim that monetary policy distorts resource allocations is generally concerned with tight money rather than with easy money.[7] At first glance this claim looks invalid, since countercyclical monetary policy serves to raise interest rates at one time and to lower interest rates at other times. The average interest rate ruling over the cycle is left essentially un-

[7] Criticisms of the allocative effects of easy money are scarce. Occasionally Federal Reserve spokesmen claim that if money is too easy banks are induced to make too many marginal loans so that the safety of the banking system is reduced, and unsound investment occurs.

affected. If so, how can it be claimed that monetary policy discriminates against certain sectors of the economy because they are more sensitive to interest rates and to credit availability? Presumably, counter-cyclical monetary policy reduces investment in these sectors at one time but raises it at other times. There are two answers to this argument. First, monetary policy, by causing countercyclical fluctuations in a sector, may increase instability for that particular sector. This hurts the factors of production employed in this sector and perhaps also hurts potential customers. Another answer takes a different approach. As is discussed in Chapter 5, one of the alternatives to counter-cyclical monetary policy is a policy of keeping interest rates low throughout the cycle. And some economists who are unwilling to go quite this far believe that the Federal Reserve has in recent years generally been too restrictive. For some observers countercyclical monetary policy has in this way become almost identified with tight money policy.

Specific Sectors

With this background let us look at the areas of the economy where monetary policy is claimed to have distorted resource allocation, starting with those sectors where this claim does not deny that monetary policy is neutral but instead asserts that neutrality is undesirable.

One of these areas is the saving-income ratio of the economy. Although there is no unanimity among economists that we should raise our rate of capital accumulation to spur economic growth, a number of economists do advocate such a policy. One way to increase capital accumulation is to make investment more profitable by lowering the interest rate. The inflationary impact of this increase in investment can then be offset by raising income taxes, which lowers consumption. By using monetary and fiscal policy, in this particular combination, investment can be increased. If one accepts this policy, the rate of interest should be kept low, and a tight money policy (which lowers investment proportionately more than consumption) is undesirable even in an inflationary period. If monetary policy is to be used to curb inflation, it should not be a neutral monetary policy but one that curbs consumption rather than investment; that is, it should consist of controls over consumer credit.

But there are three qualifications to this conclusion. First, the notion that one should raise the rate of capital accumulation is open to debate. Second, if we do decide to increase the rate of capital accumulation, a low interest rate is not the only way this can be done. Tax incentives for investment could accomplish the same purpose. Third, there is a more fundamental issue: A firm quantity theorist would argue that if the Federal Reserve increases the quantity of money to lower interest rates, prices will rise proportionately in spite of the tax increase, and this price rise then raises the real interest rate again. Fourth, the above argument refers basically to the *average* level of interest rates over the cycle. A low average interest rate is compatible with raising the interest rate during the expansion and lowering it during a contraction.

There is a closely related argument that consists of contrasting industrial plant and equipment investment with consumer credit. The argument asserts that industrial plant and equipment investment should be fostered because it contributes to economic growth; by contrast, consumer credit finances less socially desirable items. It is then pointed out that plant and equipment investment is more responsive to conventional monetary policy than is consumer credit. Hence, the argument claims, conventional monetary policy has an unfavorable resource allocation effect and should be replaced, or at least supplemented, by a different type of monetary policy, namely a revival of consumer credit controls. Whether one accepts this view depends in part on one's attitude toward a free-market system. In addition, as pointed out earlier, it is by no means certain that consumer credit is really so insensitive to a restrictive monetary policy.

A second area where monetary policy is said to hurt resource allocation is federal government finance. The Treasury is the biggest debtor in the country. Interest charges in the federal budget (excluding payments to trust funds) are now running at a rate of over $10 billion a year so that the Treasury is hurt substantially by a rise in interest rates.

Note that this argument, too, relates to the average level of interest rates and not to countercyclical monetary policy per se. Moreover, most economists would probably agree that the deadweight burden of taxes imposed to pay the higher interest rates is not so great that we should abandon a major stabilization tool merely to reduce the interest burden of the Treasury.

Third, the distribution of income provides one of the most popular criticisms of tight money policy. A high rate of interest, one argument contends, helps lenders at the expense of borrowers. Since lenders tend to be the "rich" and borrowers tend to be the "poor," tight money makes the distribution of income more unequal. Monetary policy should therefore work to keep interest rates low rather than be used as a countercyclical tool. Actually, the situation is complicated by the fact that much of the interest payments are received not by households but by financial institutions like banks and life insurance companies. When these institutions receive an increase in interest income it is hard to say how this receipt is distributed among customers and stockholders. Thus, a recent statistical study found that low income groups will gain more than high income groups if interest rates rise.[8]

Note also that if countercyclical monetary policy causes interest rates to rise at one time, it causes them to fall at others. In any case, if the federal government wants to make the distribution of income more equal, it does not have to use monetary policy for that purpose. Even if tight money were to make the distribution of income more unequal, the government could offset this by making the tax system more progressive.

Let us turn now to those sectors where monetary policy is said to cause a distortion of resource allocation because its impact is *not* neutral but is unduly great. One sector that is said to be hurt excessively by tight money—and, indeed, to bear the brunt of it—is residential construction. For example, the Council of Economic Advisers stated its belief that the effects of tight money on aggregate demand in 1966 operated primarily through the mortgage market.[9] Residential construction is a sector that is powerfully affected by changing conditions in the money market, and even observers who are not generally "cheap money men" have at times felt that monetary policy was hurting residential construction too much.[10] (Note that tight

[8] See Oswald Brownlee and Alfred Conrad, "Effects upon the Distribution of Income of a Tight Money Policy," American Economic Association, *Papers and Proceedings,* Vol. 51 (May, 1961), pp. 74–85. This paper is a summary of a much longer study done for the Commission on Money and Credit.

[9] *Economic Report of the President* (Washington, D.C.: Executive Office of the President, 1967), p. 60.

[10] For example, on July 14, 1966, all the Republican members

money reduces not only new construction but also in-hibits the sale of existing houses.)

But the mere fact that a particular sector is sensitive to monetary policy does not mean that monetary policy is not neutral. As explained above, neutrality does not mean proportionality. Since residential construction is a long-term investment one would expect it to be relatively responsive to monetary policy. In many cases, the homeowner can maximize his utility by postponing the purchase of the house until the interest rate falls. Thus the countercyclical pattern shown by residential construction should not be too surprising and is not inconsistent with the view that monetary policy is neutral. There is, however, one way in which monetary policy may fail to be neutral in its impact on residential construction. Since banks and other financial institutions ration credit, even borrowers who are willing to pay more than the prevailing interest rate may be unable to obtain mortgage financing.[11]

---

of the House Banking and Currency Committee called upon the President to appoint a committee to investigate the decline in residential construction resulting from tight money ("U.S. Stands Pat on Discount Rate," *New York Times,* July 15, 1966, p. 39).

[11] At one time it was widely believed that monetary policy was not neutral in its impact on residential construction for another reason. This is the interest rate ceiling on FHA and VA mortgages. But as new data became available it was found that the countercyclical pattern also existed for mortgages unconnected with the Federal Housing Authority or Veteran's Administration. Hence, the FHA and VA ceilings cannot be the sole cause of the countercyclical behavior, though they do appear to have some effect, particularly the VA ceiling. See Eugene Brady, "A Sectorial Econometric Study of the Postwar Residential-Housing Market," *Journal of Political Economy,* Vol. 75 (April, 1967), pp. 147–149, and Jack Guttentag, "The Short Cycle in Residential Construction," *American Economic Review,* Vol. 51 (June, 1961), pp. 275–298.

Another area in which tight money is said to have an undue effect is investment by state and local governments. A number of observers, led by John Kenneth Galbraith, believe that investment in schools and other government facilities is seriously slighted. If this contention is correct then any cutback in such investment caused by monetary policy is a serious matter. Again, since state and local government investment is long-term investment, a relatively great response to monetary policy is consistent with monetary policy being neutral. But there is one institutional factor that causes tight money to have more than a neutral effect on state and local government investment. This is that many state and local government projects have a restraint on the interest rate they may pay; bond elections and state law give the maximum rate of interest on the bonds. Thus as interest rates rise a number of state and local projects find themselves priced out of the money market. (Moreover, people who are concerned about the inadequate level of state and local investment would in many cases be concerned about a cutback in state and local investment even if it were merely a response to a neutral monetary policy. If such investment is below its optimal level, then a *neutral* policy would not maximize economic well-being. The criticism that tight money reduces state and local government investment unduly really belongs to both lines of criticism, one claiming that monetary policy is not neutral and the other that neutrality is bad.)

There are three answers to the argument that countercyclical monetary policy hurts state and local investment. First, note that this argument, too, actually relates to high interest rates over the long run rather than to a countercyclical monetary policy. Second, if state and local government investment is too low, it can be increased without making money easy for the whole economy by having the Federal government subsidize it more than at present. Third, there is a question of fact: Does a tight money policy really cut back state and local investment substantially? One study concluded that:

> . . . At no time during the period studied did a restrictive monetary policy "throttle" or severely curtail state and local capital projects. Its impact appears to have been limited to roughly the marginal 5 percent of capital projects, those having a more postponable nature.[12]

Another area where tight money is said to have an unduly harsh effect is the financial market. There are two separate problems here. First, there is the effect on the money market as a whole. Clearly, monetary policy impinges on the money market more directly than on other markets, and this effect may raise the cost curves of the financial industry. But most economists would probably agree that this cost is worth paying. Second, there is the effect on commercial banks. To be sure, they are strongly affected by monetary policy, but it is by no means clear that a tight money policy reduces their profits.

This leaves the impact of tight money on small business—one of the biggest, if not *the* biggest issue, in

[12] Frank Morris, "Impact of Monetary Policy on State and Local Governments: An Empirical Study," *Journal of Finance*, Vol. 15 (May, 1960), p. 249. Another study found that tight money caused a postponement or cutback of municipal capital expenditures by 4 to 7 percent. (See Charlotte Phelps, "The Impact of Monetary Policy on State and Local Government Expenditures in the United States," in Commission on Money and Credit, *Impacts of Monetary Policy* [Englewood Cliffs, N.J.: Prentice-Hall, 1963], p. 647.)

the debate on the allocational effect of monetary policy. As background to this debate, remember that regardless of monetary policy there is considerable concern about the difficulties that small business faces in obtaining adequate financing.

There are several reasons why tight money may impose a greater burden on small business than on large firms. First, small business is more dependent on bank financing than is large business because small firms find it very costly to float securities. Since much of the initial impact of monetary policy centers on banks, small firms who are dependent on banks may find that a restrictive monetary policy cuts their access to capital substantially. Second, it is argued that in rationing credit banks discriminate against small firms. When credit is rationed banks are more concerned with meeting the demands of their good customers than those of their weaker customers, and generally large firms meet the usual criteria of credit worthiness better than do small firms. Not only does credit rationing lead to discrimination against small firms, but it also causes discrimination against new firms since banks try to take care of the needs of their old customers before taking on new customers.

Moreover, if a large firm is denied credit by one bank it can turn to another bank, but small firms find it much more difficult to do this. Small firms have to borrow from banks in their own area since they are not known outside of it. Large firms, on the other hand, have access to banks all over the country. Also, if interest rates rise banks may find it unprofitable to lend to small firms. Interest rates on loans to small firms are higher than those on loans to large firms, so that as interest rates in general rise, the rate that can be charged to small firms may be limited at an unprofitable level by the ceiling imposed by state usury laws.[13]

But there is another side to this debate, too. Whether banks really cut back loans to small business, or whether they try to keep small customers by taking care of their needs, is still a debatable issue. One important study found no evidence of discrimination against small firms.[14]

Moreover, in a period of tight money large firms lend very substantial amounts to their smaller customers by extending trade credit. But there are two qualifications. First, trade credit is often very expensive for firms so that while the extension of trade credit itself ameliorates the impact of tight money for small firms, the very fact that so many small firms are willing to take trade credit suggests that they experience great difficulty in getting financing in a period of tight money. The second qualification is that trade credit is a competitive weapon. If small firms have difficulty in getting financing and are therefore inhibited in *extending* trade credit, they are at a competitive disadvantage vis-à-vis their larger competitors.

Thus, to summarize this whole discussion, monetary policy does seem to create some distortion in resource

[13] Another point, raised by Galbraith, is that competitive firms are unable to pass the higher cost of funds on to their customers by raising their prices. Large oligopolistic firms, on the other hand, usually have an unexploited margin of potential profit and, hence, can raise their prices and pass the higher interest costs on. (See Kenneth Galbraith, "Market Structure and Stabilization Policy," *Review of Economics and Statistics,* Vol. 39 [May, 1957], pp. 124–133.)

[14] See G. L. Bach and C. J. Huizenga, "The Differential Effects of Tight Money," *American Economic Review,* Vol. 51 (March, 1961), pp. 52–80. Note, however, that this study has been subjected to considerable criticism. See the debate in the *American Economic Review,* Vol. 51 (December, 1961), pp. 1039–1044, and Vol. 53 (September, 1963), pp. 740–745.

allocation from what it otherwise would be but does so to a much smaller extent than many critics of monetary policy allege. Three questions emerge in this connection: first, are the distorting effects so serious that a restrictive monetary policy should be avoided? Second, are the distortions so small that it would be feasible to use monetary policy much more vigorously than we have done in the past? Third, does monetary policy create fewer distortions than fiscal policy? Different people will read the evidence presented above differently. Probably the majority of monetary economists would answer the first question in the negative. Whether the majority would answer the second question in the affirmative and would favor a much stronger monetary policy is hard to say since this depends also on the timing of monetary policy. The third question, which concerns the relative distortions of monetary and fiscal policy, is a question extremely hard to answer since it depends upon the type of fiscal policy being considered as well as on one's value judgments.

Chapter **5** | **Alternative Monetary Policies**

The previous chapters have discussed the goals and methods of monetary policy as well as its strength, its resource allocation effects, and its timing. This material can now be combined by considering different monetary policies that have been proposed, or, more specifically, different evaluations of the desirability of countercyclical monetary policy. Obviously it is not possible to consider all possible policy views here; instead this chapter deals with four policy positions. One is the position currently taken by the Federal Reserve, another is that of the advocates of easy money, a third is that of the monetarists, and the fourth is the proposal to replace countercyclical monetary policy with a policy of increasing the money supply at a constant rate regardless of the business cycle. These four different outlooks comprise the positions of the great majority of economists, though there are substantial points of disagreement even among supporters of the same general position, and many economists take an in-between view. The policy positions described below are therefore, in most cases, not those of any single individual or institution but are an amalgam of fairly similar views.

But before coming to the disagreements, we should note that there is substantial agreement on one important issue; that is, financial panics should be prevented. Traditionally, this has been an important task of monetary policy, though nowadays deposit insurance has taken over much of this task. There is little discussion on the issue, in part because there is widespread agreement on it and in part because most economists feel that financial panics are a thing of the past.[1]

The Dominant View

The label "dominant view" is not really an ideal description; the term "establishment view" would be better if it were not for the fact that the term "establishment" is so often used in a derogatory sense. In any case, the policy to be described in this section is the one favored by the Federal Reserve as well as by many economists and by what the newspapers call "the financial community."

In this view, the average level of interest rates over the business cycle is not very important—what is important is that interest rates and credit availability should behave countercyclically. By using monetary policy in a countercyclical fashion the Federal Reserve can moderate the business cycle. To be sure, interest rates and credit availability may not be the most important factors impinging on the businessman's decision to invest, but they do have a significant effect. Monetary policy may not be strong enough to do the whole stabilizing task by itself—particularly if fluctua-

[1] But for a less sanguine view see Hyman Minsky, "Financial Crisis, Financial Systems and the Performance of the Economy," in Commission on Money and Credit, *Private Capital Markets* (Englewood Cliffs, N.J.: Prentice-Hall, 1964), pp. 173–380.

tions are severe—and may have to be supplemented by countercyclical fiscal policy. But all the same, monetary policy should be operated in a counter-cyclical manner so that it contributes as much as possible to stabilization and balance-of-payments equilibrium. Granted that monetary policy does not have its main impact on income immediately and that its effectiveness may be reduced to some extent by lags, monetary policy is still fast enough to be stabilizing rather than destabilizing.

On the whole, the resource allocation effects of a countercyclical monetary policy are not very unfavorable. When advocates of easy money disparage the resource allocation effects of tight money they are really complaining about the way in which a free market allocates a scarce resource and are attempting to impose their social priorities on the economy. As a nation America has, on the whole, chosen to let resource allocation be guided by free market processes. Monetary policy should not be used to upset this decision.

Moreover, the argument runs, at least in the Federal Reserve's variant, since tax increases are politically unpopular, the alternative to tight money is usually inflation, and inflation distorts resource allocation and income distribution much more than tight money does. Not only is inflation an evil in and of itself, but an inflation makes the subsequent recession more severe and, hence, increases the over-all level of unemployment over the cycle as well as worsening the balance-of-payments problem.[2]

This fear of inflation, one should note, is widespread

[2] As Federal Reserve Chairman Martin said: "I think one of the reasons we have had so much unemployment as we have had, and you may think this is silly, is because we have had too easy money." (Cited in John Culbertson, *Full Employment or Stagnation?* [New York: McGraw-Hill], p. 156.)

in the financial community and is an important component of the dominant view. But note that many economists who, on the whole, accept the dominant view do not share the Federal Reserve's great fear of inflation, and lay more stress on full employment, and less on price stability, than does the Federal Reserve.

In the dominant view monetary policy should "lean against the wind." In doing so, it should concern itself with many such variables as the stock of money, interest rates, credit conditions, and the volume and quality of bank credit. All of these variables are important, and policy has to be based on a mature judgment regarding the over-all pattern they indicate. In arriving at such a judgment, the level of interest rates can be used as a good indicator of the current posture of monetary policy.

The Monetarist Countercyclical Policy

Many economists accept the above point of view in one respect; they believe that countercyclical monetary policy is desirable. However, they differ sharply from the Federal Reserve in the type of countercyclical policy they advocate.

To the countercyclical "monetarists" the stock of money is the critical variable the Federal Reserve should look at. Instead of concerning itself with interest rates, credit conditions, and so forth, the Federal Reserve should ensure that the stock of money grows at the proper rate—that is, slower in the expansion than during the recession. This statement might seem innocuous. After all, doesn't "leaning against the wind" imply managing the stock of money this way? But as we pointed out in Chapter 1, using the conventional definition of money, the Federal Reserve has not thus regulated the money stock. In recent cycles, the stock of money has increased faster in the expansion than in the recession, suggesting that the Federal Reserve was leaning *with* the wind. The monetarist explains this by the fact that the Federal Reserve has been paying too much attention to the absolute level of interest rates, to free reserves, and so forth. A policy that tends to stabilize the interest rate causes destabilizing changes in the growth rate of the money stock. During the expansion, as the marginal efficiency of investment and economic activity in general rise, interest rates tend to rise, too. This rise in the interest rate reduces expenditures and, hence, tends to limit the expansion. Conversely, during a recession when activity falls, the interest rate declines, tending to limit the recession. But if the Federal Reserve is concerned with interest rate stability, it will attempt to limit interest rate changes by allowing the money stock to grow at a more rapid rate in the expansion when interest rates are rising than in the contraction when they are falling. This means that it introduces a *procyclical* element into the growth of the money stock. To the monetarist what is important is not the rate of interest per se, but only the rate of interest *relative to the marginal efficiency of investment*. For example, during a recession a discount rate of 4 percent may represent a restrictive monetary policy. If the Treasury bill rate were, say, 3 percent, banks would tend to repay borrowing and keep a relatively large volume of excess reserves. Conversely, during an expansion a 5 percent discount rate may be an easy money policy. If the Treasury bill rate is, say, 6 percent, a 5 percent discount rate would give banks an incentive to borrow and to keep only a low level of excess reserves, both factors tending to raise the money stock.

Now the Federal Reserve no longer explicitly considers interest stabilization to be one of its major goals, but according to the monetarists, its policies work in the direction of interest stabilization for three reasons. First, one of the criteria used by the Federal Reserve in deciding whether its current monetary policy is expansionary is the ease with which borrowers can obtain bank loans at the prevailing rate of interest. But if the rate of interest is high, the fact that banks are ready to make loans at this high rate does not show that money is easy but indicates instead that money is tight.[3] Moreover, the current level of the interest rate must be related not to previous levels of the interest rate but rather to the marginal efficiency of investment.

Second, in a recession the Federal Reserve is sometimes reluctant to let the interest rate fall very much because it thinks that very low interest rates and what it terms "excessive" availability of credit, a so-called "sloppy money market," would tempt banks into making "unsound" loans.[4] To the monetarist this concern with the quality of credit is unwarranted. Bank ex-

[3] See Culbertson, *op. cit.*, Ch. 12.

[4] This argument has a long history. In its early days the Federal Reserve was bound to the real-bills doctrine that stabilization depended not on the quantity of money but on the quality of bank loans. Interest rates should be kept fairly stable and the money stock should be allowed to increase during the expansion when the demand for short-term self-liquidating business loans increases. The Federal Reserve says that it has abandoned these ideas; its critics claim to find their residue affecting current policies.

Apart from concern about a sloppy money market the Federal Reserve believes that if the reserve base is expanded too much in the recession, it will be difficult to mop up these reserves in the upswing. Moreover, the Federal Reserve has asserted that at low interest rates investment is quite interest inelastic.

amination can ensure the safety of the banking system, and the Federal Reserve should concern itself with the quantity of money.

To the Federal Reserve the monetarist case is oversimplified. It ignores the complexity of the money market, it assumes that all that matters is the quantity of money and not the interest rate, and also it misinterprets Federal Reserve policy.[5]

The Easy Money Position

A third position on monetary policy is that of the advocates of easy money. This view has significant support in Congress and among borrowers. It also represents the position of quite a number of economists. According to this view countercyclical monetary policy is desirable with one important limitation: Interest rates should not be allowed to rise to high levels at any time. The Federal Reserve should keep interest rates low and credit readily available throughout the cycle with interest rates being pushed below their average during the expansion. In other words, this position favors countercyclical monetary policy with one important restraint: Really tight money must be avoided. The degree of emphasis placed on this restraint and the willingness of abandoning it in special circumstances varies among advocates of the easy money view, but they are united in their dislike of tight money.

The easy money case consists of three components. First, there is the argument that inflation is often the result not of excess demand, but of excessive income

[5] For a good example of this type of reply by a Federal Reserve official see the statement of Governor George Mitchell before the House Banking and Currency Committee (U.S. House Committee on Banking and Currency Hearings, *The Federal Reserve System after Fifty Years*, Vol. 3 [Washington, D.C.: 88th Congress, Second Session, 1964], pp. 1955–1958).

claims by the factors of production—labor being the villain to conservatives and business oligopolists being the culprit for liberals. If inflation is the result of a so-called "cost push" rather than "demand pull," the argument claims, monetary policy is unable to prevent it. If money is tightened and aggregate demand falls, employment rather than the price level is affected. A tight money policy creates unemployment, not price stability. To be sure, if aggregate demand is reduced sufficiently the rise in unemployment and in excess capacity will *eventually* put a stop to wage and price increases, but since these factors will be effective only at a level of unemployment that is socially unacceptable, tight money is not a useful weapon against inflation.

Some easy money advocates would go even further than this and argue that an increase in interest rates raises prices by increasing the cost of production so that tight money is really inflationary. Although this argument is sometimes heard in Congress, it has little support among economists, in good part because interest is a minor element of the current cost of production.

The second component of the easy money argument is that tight money has many serious disadvantages. By reducing investment rather than consumption it reduces the rate of growth. Moreover, tight money discriminates against particular industries and makes the distribution of income more unequal. These are points discussed in some detail in Chapter 4 and so are not discussed here. Suffice it to say that advocates of easy money, unlike the supporters of the dominant view, consider the discriminatory effects of tight money to be substantial and attach a great deal of importance to them.

Some proponents of the easy money view argue

that though tight money, if carried far enough, would be able to stop inflation, even a quite substantial increase in interest rates may have little effect on aggregate spending. The marginal efficiency of investment is interest inelastic, and velocity can easily increase as interest rates rise. Moreover, lags inhibit the efficient operation of a countercyclical monetary policy. Hence, unfavorable income distribution effects of tight money are not balanced by a favorable performance as an economic stabilizer. Tight money is not the answer even to a demand-induced inflation.

Some other supporters of the easy money position take a different view and believe that tight money has a powerful—and unfortunate—effect on output. If the Federal Reserve adopts a strong tight money policy during the period of expansion it is likely to carry this policy too far and to maintain it for too long. The effect of this is to bring on a recession. Monetary policy is a very dangerous tool. A number of observers feel that the Federal Reserve has a deflationary bias, that it attaches much too much importance to price stability and much too little importance to full employment. According to this view an unwarranted fear of inflation has led the Federal Reserve to adopt policies that have sharply reduced the growth rate and thus have imposed a substantial cost on the economy.

To many adherents of the easy money position the Federal Reserve's deflationary bias is no accident; they look upon the Federal Reserve as being the representative of financial interests. Five of the voting members of the Federal Open Market Committee come from the twelve Federal Reserve Banks, and two-thirds of the directors of these Federal Reserve Banks are elected by commercial bankers. Moreover, until recently, the members of the Board of Governors tended to come from the financial community. In recent years there has been a quite radical change: At present (1967) four of the seven members of the Board of Governors are professional economists, and only one of the other members is a former banker. Moreover, the Federal Reserve has frequently said that when a commercial banker takes office at a Federal Reserve Bank he looks upon himself as representing the public interest rather than the interest of the banking community. But the problem of excessive banker influence at the Federal Reserve goes deeper than that. It has frequently been observed that a government agency set up to regulate an industry tends to become too sympathetic to the industry and frequently protects the industry against the consumer and other government agencies. This is not the result of any ill will or malfeasance. It is not surprising that officials who deal primarily with the problems of a specific industry and talk to a large extent to members of that industry will sooner or later tend to adopt the point of view of that industry. Many critics of the Federal Reserve feel that this is what has happened to it.

The main line of criticism that can be directed at the easy money approach is to challenge its basic factual suppositions. There is considerable question whether inflation is usually cost induced rather than demand induced, but this topic cannot be discussed here. Moreover, as was pointed out in Chapter 3, one can make a case that monetary policy is powerful. The argument that monetary policy has unfavorable effects on resource allocation was discussed in Chapter 4.

Rules Versus Authorities

The fourth and last major position on monetary policy is one developed many years ago at the Uni-

versity of Chicago by the late Henry Simons; its leading present-day exponent is Milton Friedman. But, in
addition to many members of the so-called "Chicago
School," a number of other economists, like James W.
Angell, Edward Shaw, and Clark Warburton, have
accepted this position in broad outline, though they
differ on a number of important points from Friedman; and it has also found an echo in Congress.[6] Since
the Friedman version of this proposal has received
most attention, this section deals primarily with his
variant of the plan.

In brief, the proposal is to abandon discretionary
monetary policy and instead to follow a so-called
"rule" that is a policy of increasing the money stock
at a constant rate each month regardless of the stage
of the business cycle. The money stock is defined by
Friedman to include time deposits in commercial

[6] In its Report on the 1967 Economic Report of the President,
the Majority of the Joint Economic Committee urged "that
the monetary authorities adopt the policy of moderate and
relatively steady increases in the money supply, avoiding the
disrupting effects of wide swings in the rate of increase or
decrease. . . . Such rate of increase should be more or less
consistent with the projected rate of growth—generally within
a range of 3–5 percent per year." The Minority had a similar
statement: "We therefore recommend that the Federal Reserve
increase the money supply in 1967 at an annual rate of 2 to 4
percent. Monetary growth should vary between the upper and
the lower end of this range, as economic conditions indicate,
but we urge the Federal Reserve to avoid the extremes of
1965 and 1966." U. S. Congress Joint Economic Committee,
Report on the January 1967 Economic Report of the President
(90th Congress, First Session, Washington, D.C., 1967), pp.
14 and 60.

For a discussion of the Chicago School which provides an
excellent background to the "rules vs. authorities" debate, see
the following three short papers: Henry Miller, Jr., "On the
'Chicago School of Economics'," *Journal of Political Economy*,
Vol. 70 (February, 1962), pp. 64–69; George Stigler, "On
the 'Chicago School of Economics': Comment," *ibid.*, pp. 70–
71; and Martin Bronfenbrenner, "Observations on the 'Chicago
School(s)'," *ibid.*, pp. 72–75.

banks, but this is not essential; the same *rule* could be applied to the money stock as conventionally defined (currency plus demand deposits). If the money stock is to be increased at a steady rate monetary policy cannot be used to counter balance-of-payments disequilibrium. Friedman advocates that the balance of payments be kept in equilibrium in another way, namely by a system of flexible exchange rates. He advocates adoption of 100 percent reserve banking, but while it would facilitate the operation of his system it is not necessary for it.

Friedman's case for increasing the money stock at a constant rate runs as follows. As a quantity theorist, he believes that after making allowance for the trend in velocity (induced by the rise of real income), changes in income mirror changes in the money stock. Hence, if the money stock is increased at a constant rate, there will be relatively few fluctuations in income. To be sure, not all fluctuations in income are due to fluctuations in money growth, so that adoption of the rule would not eliminate *all* fluctuations. But since much instability of income and particularly the more severe fluctuations are due to instability in the money growth rate, the rule would give greater income stability than the country experiences now.

But can one not do better than the rule? Granted that the abolition of discretionary policy would prevent monetary management from adding to the instability of the economy, can one not use discretionary monetary policy to reduce the instability introduced by other factors? Friedman's answer is "No," for two reasons. First, there is the problem of lags. If monetary policy takes a long and unknown time to have its main effect on income, a countercyclical monetary policy may be destabilizing. "Leaning today against next year's wind is hardly an easy task in the present

stage of meteorology." [7] Second, there is the problem
of divergent goals. Since discretionary monetary policy
has several potentially conflicting goals, like full employment and balance-of-payments equilibrium, there
is always the danger that the Federal Reserve will be
diverted from its goal of stabilization of the domestic
economy. One classic example of this type of thing
occurred in the postwar period when the Federal Reserve followed an easy money policy at a time of
inflation in order to maintain the price of government
securities at par.

Given both the less than perfect devotion of the
Federal Reserve to its goal of domestic economic stability and the difficulties of determining the correct
policy in the face of long and variable lags, one would
not be surprised to find that, in the past, the Federal
Reserve has been a destabilizing influence rather than
a stabilizing one. And, the argument runs, when one
looks at the history of the Federal Reserve one does
find that it has been perverse more frequently than
not. The money stock has been more unstable in the
years following the establishment of the Federal Reserve System in 1914 than in prior years for which we
have adequate data (1867–1914). According to Friedman a monetary rule would therefore have been preferable.[8]

> The simple rule would have avoided the excessive ex-
> pansion of the stock of money from 1919 to 1920 and
> the very sharp contraction thereafter, the fairly mild
> but steady deflationary pressure of the late 1920's, the
> collapse of the stock of money from 1929 to 1933, the
> rather rapid rise thereafter, and the sharp decline in the
> course of the 1937–38 recession. In the period since

[7] Milton Friedman, *A Program for Monetary Stability* (New
York: Fordham University Press, 1960), p. 93.
[8] *Ibid.*, pp. 93–94.

World War II, the simple rule would have produced a
lower rate of growth in the stock of money until the
end of 1946 than was in fact realized, almost the same
rate of growth during 1947, a faster rate of growth
from sometime in 1947 to the end of 1949, which is
to say, throughout the closing phases of the 1946–48
expansion and the whole of the 1948–49 contraction.

Given this inferior record of discretionary policy,
Friedman concludes that:

> In light of experience, the most urgent need is not to
> have some everpresent back-seat driver who is going to
> be continually correcting the driver's steering, but to
> get off the road the man who has been giving the car
> a shove from one side to the other all the time and
> making it difficult for the actual driver to keep it on the
> straight and narrow path. . . . I am tempted to para-
> phrase what Colin Clark once wrote about the case for
> free trade. Like other academicians, I am accustomed
> to being met with the refrain, "It's all right in theory but
> it won't work in practice." Aside from the questionable
> logic of the remark in general, in this instance almost
> the reverse of what is intended is true. There is little
> to be said in theory for the rule that the money supply
> should grow at a constant rate. The case for it is entirely
> that it would work in practice. . . .[9]

In addition to this argument that the Federal Reserve's record is worse than the rule, there are two
other arguments for the rule. One is that a rule involves less government interference with the economy
than does a discretionary policy. Professor Friedman
attaches a great deal of importance to limiting govern-

[9] The first part of this quotation is from Professor Friedman's
testimony before the Joint Economic Committee. United States
Congress, Joint Economic Committee, *Employment, Growth,
and Price Levels, Hearings* (Washington, D.C., 1959), p. 615.
The second part is from his *A Program for Monetary Stability,
op. cit.,* p. 98.

ment controls. The other argument is that a monetary rule would create confidence. If businessmen know that the money stock will be increased at a steady rate they will *expect* stability, and this will facilitate the maintenance of stability. For example, during a recession businessmen would know that demand will be depressed for a short time only and, hence, would not cut back on investment as much as they would under the current system.

The rate at which the money stock should be increased each year is given by Professor Friedman as 4 or 5 percent, if money is defined to include time deposits in commercial banks, and as 3 percent if time deposits are excluded. A 4 percent increase in the money stock would offset the projected 3 percent rate of increase in physical output and the 1 percent secular decline in velocity. But Friedman is not very much concerned with the precise rate of increase selected as long as it is maintained steadily. If the rate of increase of the money stock exceeds the rate at which output is growing and velocity is declining there will be *secular* inflation. But as long as prices rise steadily the inflation will be predictable and, hence, will do less harm. All wages, debts, and other contracts could be adjusted for this expected increase in prices so that inflation would not redistribute income. Conversely, if output grows at a rate faster than 3 percent, or if *velocity* declines at a rate greater than 1 percent, the rule will result in a falling price level. Friedman feels that this, too, would be acceptable; contracts could be written to make allowance for this drop in prices and, hence, it would not create a serious problem. While he believes that, on the whole, price stability is preferable to a *secular* trend in prices, his main concern is to avoid *fluctuations* in the price level, not a steady trend. The monetary rule is not necessarily a rule of price level stability.

But these arguments favoring a rule are accepted only by a minority of economists. A number of points have been raised by the supporters of discretionary policy.[10] One point is political. Quite apart from the technical reasons of lags, and so forth, proponents of the rule frequently claim that a monetary rule would limit government interference. To some of the opponents of the rule this great antipathy toward government regulation seems unwarranted.[11] A second point is that past experience with an automatic rule has not been very encouraging. As Jacob Viner has put it:

> In the economic field important rules affecting important social issues have in fact been extremely scarce, and to the extent that they have had a substantial degree of durability this has been largely explicable either by the fact that they evolved into taboos, or ends in themselves, and were thus removed from the area of open discussion and rational appraisal, or by the tolerance of widespread evasion. The most conspicuous instances of economic rules with a substantial degree of durability were the prohibition of lending at interest and the maintenance of fixed monetary standards in terms of precious metals. The most enthusiastic advocate of rules can de-

---

[10] The leading publications criticizing the rule are: Abba Lerner, "Review of Milton Friedman, *A Program for Monetary Stability*," *Journal of the American Statistical Association*, Vol. 57 (March, 1962), pp. 211–220; Jacob Viner, "The Necessity and Desirable Range of Discretion to be Allowed to a Monetary Authority," in Leland Yeager (ed.), *In Search of a Monetary Constitution* (Cambridge, Mass.: Harvard University Press, 1962), pp. 244–274; and Daniel Ahearn, *Federal Reserve Policy Reappraised* (New York: Columbia University Press, 1963), pp. 225–233.

[11] Viner has argued along a different line, namely that government control is control regardless of whether it takes the form of a rule or of discretion (*ibid.*, pp. 244–245).

rive little comfort from the availability of these historical precedents.[12]

Moreover, there is the problem that monetary policy has a plurality of goals. To Friedman this plurality is unwelcome, and one of the reasons for his advocacy of the rule is precisely the fact that he thinks it is better to give monetary policy a single task rather than to let various goals pull it in various directions. But to other economists, the existence of multiple goals provides a reason for opposing a rule. If one considers the four goals stated at the beginning of this book to be desirable and achievable only by monetary policy, then the adoption of a rule may involve the loss of economic well-being. To illustrate by just one example: To advocates of fixed exchange rates, a monetary rule would have a great disadvantage—it would prevent the use of monetary policy to adjust the balance of payments.

On a more technical level, economists have questioned Friedman's belief in long and variable lags in the effect of monetary policy and, therefore, his view that discretionary monetary policy is destabilizing. Moreover, there is a problem about the definition of money. If liquid assets, like savings and loan shares, are important in determining expenditures or should become so in the future, a monetary rule may do little good. As one critic has put it, "If a fixed rule had in the early 1800's fixed a regular percentage increase in the supply of banknotes—the major component of the money supply at the time—the rule would have become largely irrelevant with the emergence of demand deposits as the major type of money.[13]

A number of criticisms have focused on the com-

[12] *Ibid.*, p. 248.
[13] Ahearn, *op. cit.*, p. 226.

patibility of the rule with future requirements. For example, suppose that velocity should decrease at a faster rate in the future or that productivity should increase at a faster rate. Given the rule, full employment would then require falling prices—but are prices flexible enough to allow a declining price level to co-exist with full employment? Friedman believes that the answer is yes and points to the rapid increase in output during the 1870's when the price level fell substantially. But probably the majority of economists would feel that whatever may have been true in the 1870's, at present there is so much price rigidity that inadequate aggregate demand is more likely to result in a fall in output than a fall in prices.[14]

A related point is that velocity may decline irregularly or potential output may grow at an unstable rate. If so, given full employment, a constant rate of growth of the money stock would result in an irregular price movement. If so, some of the benefit of the rule would be lost since businessmen's price expectations could be destabilizing. This consideration suggests the use of something in between a rigid rule and discretion. This is to adjust the money stock for changes in potential output and in velocity during the previous period.[15] Moreover, if, as some economists believe, we face a situation of secular cost-push inflation, then the monetary rule would require substantial unemployment.

A central issue in the whole dispute is the efficiency of the Federal Reserve. Opponents of the rule, while conceding past errors by the Federal Reserve, have

[14] On the other side of the stability line, there is probably more support for the proposition that a predictable inflation would do no harm.

[15] See Martin Bronfenbrenner, "Monetary Rules: A New Look," *Journal of Law and Economics,* Vol. 8 (October, 1965), pp. 173–194.

argued that the Federal Reserve is unlikely to repeat such errors in the future. The fact that a child cannot be trusted to drive a car does not mean that an adult should not be allowed to drive. Thus, what is relevant is not the successes or failures of the Federal Reserve since 1914 but its successes or failures in recent years.

For the postwar period several studies have attempted to evaluate discretionary monetary policy and to compare it to the monetary rule.[16] They have computed the stock of money required to maintain price stability and full employment and have compared this to both the actual increase in the money stock and the increase which would have resulted under the monetary rule. A study by Martin Bronfenbrenner ended by advocating a modified rule in which the money stock is increased at a rate depending on the previous year's increase in potential output and decrease in velocity; another study by Franco Modigliani found discretion superior to a rule. But both of these studies are subject to the criticism that they make inadequate allowance for the lag of monetary policy so that they are testing Friedman's proposal by assuming away an important part, perhaps the most important part, of his case.

But note that most of these critcisms merely point out why a rule would not work well. Most of them do not focus on the basic case for the rule, namely that long and unpredictable lags may make countercyclical monetary policy destabilizing. As was pointed

[16] See Bronfenbrenner, "Statistical Tests of Rival Monetary Rules," *Journal of Political Economy*, Vol. 69 (February, 1961), pp. 1–14, and "Statistical Tests of Rival Monetary Rules: Quarterly Data Supplement," *Journal of Political Economy*, Vol. 69 (December, 1961), pp. 621–625; Franco Modigliani, "Some Empirical Tests of Monetary Management and of Rules vs. Discretion," *Journal of Political Economy*, Vol. 72 (June, 1964), pp. 211–245.

out in Chapter 4, relatively little is known about the length and variability of the lag, and economists *may* therefore at the present time not really be in a position to decide the rules versus authorities issue.

Moreover, there is another difficult problem. In recent years our knowledge of monetary policy has grown significantly. There has been a substantial upsurge in work on monetary economics, both within the Federal Reserve and in universities. Even if long and unpredictable lags make an effective counter-cyclical policy impossible to operate now, in time economists may learn to predict the lag for individual cases and, thus, to base monetary policy on a forecast. Whether or not America will reach this stage in the foreseeable future is hard, if not impossible, to say.[17]

[17] Friedman has suggested that the government should now adopt a monetary rule that it could abandon once it learned enough about monetary policy. But a danger of this proposal is that if discretionary monetary policy is abandoned, the government may not get back to it readily later on.

Further Reading

The following short selection is fairly general. For references on specific points, see the bibliographical footnotes in my Monetary Policy in the United States *(New York: Random House, in preparation).*

General Works

Ahearn, Daniel. *Federal Reserve Policy Reappraised, 1951–59.* New York: Columbia University Press, 1963.

Cagan, Phillip. "A Commentary on Some Current Issues in the Theory of Monetary Policy," in Michael Brennen (ed.), *Patterns of Market Behavior.* Providence, R.I.: Brown University Press, 1965.

Commission on Money and Credit. *Money and Credit.* Englewood Cliffs, N.J.: Prentice-Hall, 1961, Chs. 1–3.

———. *Impacts of Monetary Policy.* Englewood Cliffs, N.J.: Prentice-Hall, 1963.

———. *Stabilization Policies.* Englewood Cliffs, N.J.: Prentice-Hall, 1963.

———. *Monetary Management.* Englewood Cliffs, N.J.: Prentice-Hall, 1963.

Culbertson, John. *Full Employment or Stagnation?* New York: McGraw-Hill, 1964.

Friedman, Milton. *A Program for Monetary Stability.* New York: Fordham University Press, 1960.

Goldenweiser, Emanuel. *Monetary Management.* New York: McGraw-Hill, 1951.

Horwich, George (ed.). *Monetary Process and Policy: A Symposium.* Homewood, Ill.: Irwin, 1967.

Jacoby, Neil (ed.). *United States Monetary Policy.* New York: Praeger, 1964.

Johnson, Harry. "Monetary Theory and Policy," *American Economic Review,* Vol. 52 (June, 1962), pp. 335–384.

U.S. Board of Governors of the Federal Reserve System. *The Federal Reserve System: Purposes and Function.* Washington, D.C., 1963.

U.S. Congress, Joint Economic Committee. *Staff Report on Employment, Growth and Price Levels.* 86th Congress, First Session, Washington, D.C., 1959, Ch. 9.

Viner, Jacob. "Problems of Monetary Control," from *Essays in International Finance, #45,* International Finance Section, Princeton University. Princeton, N.J., International Finance Section, 1964.

Warburton, Clark. *Depression, Inflation and Monetary Policy, Selected Papers, 1945–53.* Baltimore: Johns Hopkins University Press, 1966.

Goals

Eastburn, D. P. *The Federal Reserve on Record.* Philadelphia: Federal Reserve Bank of Philadelphia, n.d., pp. 15–27.

Klein, L. R., and R. G. Bodkin. "Empirical Aspects of the Trade-Offs among Three Goals: High Level Employment, Price Stability and Economic Growth," in Commission on Money and Credit, *Inflation, Growth and Employment.* Englewood Cliffs, N.J.: Prentice-Hall, 1964, pp. 367–428.

Rothwell, J. C. "Aiming at a Moving Target," Federal Reserve Bank of Philadelphia, *Business Review* (April, 1964), pp. 3–19.

Scitovsky, T. and A. "Inflation versus Unemployment: An Examination of their Effects," in Commission on Money and Credit, *Inflation, Growth and Employment, op. cit.,* pp. 429–470.

Tools

Aschheim, Joseph. *Techniques of Monetary Control.* Baltimore: Johns Hopkins Press, 1961.

Brunner, Karl, and Allan Meltzer. *Some General Features of the Federal Reserve's Approach to Policy, The Federal Reserve's Attachment to the Free Reserve Concept,* and *An Alternative Approach to the Monetary Mechanism.* U.S. Congress, House Banking and Currency Committee, 88th Congress, 2nd Session, Washington, D.C., 1964.

Guttentag, Jack. "The Strategy of Open Market Operations," *Quarterly Journal of Economics,* Vol. 80 (February, 1966), pp. 1–30.

Roosa, Robert. *Federal Reserve Operations in the Money and Government Securities Market.* New York: Federal Reserve Bank of New York, 1956.

Smith, Warren. "The Discount Rate as a Credit Control Weapon," *Journal of Political Economy,* Vol. 66 (April, 1958), pp. 171–177.

———. "Instruments of General Monetary Control," *National Banking Review,* Vol. 1 (September, 1963), pp. 47–76.

———. "Reserve Requirements in the American Monetary System," in Commission on Money and Credit, *Monetary Management.* Englewood Cliffs, N.J.: Prentice-Hall, 1963, pp. 175–315.

Zupnick, Elliot. "Consumer Credit and Monetary Policy in the United States and the United Kingdom," *Journal of Finance,* Vol. 17 (May, 1962), pp. 342–354.

Strength of Monetary Policy

Crockett, Jean, Irwin Friend, and Henry Shavell. "The Impact of Monetary Stringency on Business Investment," *Survey of Current Business,* Vol. 47 (August, 1967), pp. 10–27.

Gurley, John, and Edward Shaw. "Financial Aspects of Economic Development," *American Economic Review,* Vol. 45 (September, 1955), pp. 515–538.

Lindbeck, Assar. *The "New" Theory of Credit Control in the United States.* Uppsala, Sweden: Almquist and Wiksell, 1962.

Minsky, Hyman. "Central Banking and Money Market Changes," *Quarterly Journal of Economics,* Vol. 71 (May, 1957), pp. 171–187.

Ritter, Lawrence. "Income Velocity and Anti-Inflationary Monetary Policy," *American Economic Review,* Vol. 49 (March, 1959), pp. 120–129.

Smith, Warren. "On the Effectiveness of Monetary Policy," *American Economic Review,* Vol. 46 (September, 1956), pp. 588–606.

———. "Financial Intermediaries and Monetary Controls," *Quarterly Journal of Economics,* Vol. 73 (November, 1959), pp. 533–553.

The Efficiency of Monetary Policy

Bach, G. L., and C. J. Huizenga. "The Differential Effects of
Tight Money," *American Economic Review,* Vol. 51
(March, 1961), pp. 52–80. See also the critical comments
by Deane Carson (*American Economic Review,* Vol. 51
[December, 1961], pp. 1039–1042) and Dale Tussing
(*ibid.,* Vol. 53 [September, 1963], pp. 740–743) and the
replies by G. L. Bach and C. J. Huizenga, which follow
these papers.

Fand, David, and Ira Scott, Jr. "The Recent Questioning of
Monetary Policy," *Current Economic Comment,* Vol. 21
(August, 1959), pp. 17–28.

Friedman, Milton. "The Effects of a Full Employment Policy
on Economic Stability: A Formal Analysis," in his *Essays
in Positive Economics.* Chicago: University of Chicago
Press, 1953.

Schlesinger, James. "Monetary Policy and Its Critics," *Journal
of Political Economy,* Vol. 68 (December, 1960), pp.
601–616.

Alternative Policies

Bronfenbrenner, Martin. "Monetary Rules: A New Look,"
Journal of Law and Economics, Vol. 8 (October, 1965),
pp. 173–194.

Culbertson, John. "The Use of Monetary Policy," *Southern
Economic Journal,* Vol. 28 (October, 1961), pp. 130–137.

Friedman, Milton. Testimony before the Joint Economic Com-
mittee, *Employment, Growth, and Price Levels, Hearings,*
May 25–28, 1959. Washington, D.C., 86th Congress, First
Session, 1959. See also his above listed *A Program for
Monetary Stability.*

Lerner, Abba. "Review of Milton Friedman, *A Program for
Monetary Stability,*" *Journal of the American Statistical
Association,* Vol. 57 (March, 1962), pp. 211–220.

Selden, Richard. "Stable Money Growth," in Leland Yeager
(ed.), *In Search of a Monetary Constitution.* Cambridge:
Harvard University Press, 1962, pp. 322–355.

Simons, Henry. "Rules vs. Authorities in Monetary Policy," re-
printed in American Economic Association, *Readings in
Monetary Theory.* Homewood, Ill.: Irwin, 1951, pp. 337–
368.

Viner, Jacob. "The Necessity and Desirable Range of Discretion to be Allowed to a Monetary Authority," in Leland Yeager (ed.), *In Search of a Monetary Constitution*. Cambridge: Harvard University Press, 1962, pp. 244–275.

Index